"I was alw  This
has helpe(
Janis K., L

"Learning these tips from a woman is the best thing to happen for men! Stevens and Wunder have put together a book that not only contains great information about pleasing a woman, but also addresses the subject with sensitivity and depth. This book really shows that making love doesn't only take place physically, it takes place emotionally as well. Great book for anyone who really wants to love their woman!"
Craig W., Asheville, NC

"My wife is so happy!"
Jack R., Asheville, NC

"I was lucky to read a trial copy, and all I can say is, thanks for this honest work. My girlfriend and I are both smiling!"
Ben S., Charlotte, NC

"I thought the G-spot and female ejaculation were myths. Boy, was I wrong."
Sandy W., Lexington, KY

"I always wanted to try adult toys, but was too embarrassed. I was also afraid that my husband would think he wasn't man enough for my needs. After reading this manual together, he brought me home a couple of surprises that we both have fun using on each other. Thanks so much."
Leslie D., Lake Placid, FL

A Note to You,
the Reader

This book is an excerpt from *How To Be A Happy Lesbian: A Coming Out Guide*. Because it is being marketed to everyone who loves and has primary sexual relationships with women–lesbians, straight men, transgendered people, and bisexual women and men–it has been revised and has more inclusive language. Instead of using both pronouns, which can be irritating to say the least, we have opted to switch pronoun use so that everyone feels included. The only information that is different in this book than in *How To Be A Happy Lesbian: A Coming Out Guide* is the description of how STDs affect men's anatomy.

If you are a little uncomfortable purchasing this book today, it is also available on the Web. You may purchase the soft cover edition to be sent directly to you, or a downloadable PDF file, which you can read in privacy on your computer. There are complete instructions on how to do this at:

www.amazingdreamspublishing.com

LESBIAN SEX TIPS

A Guide for Anyone Who Wants to Bring Pleasure to The Woman She (Or He) Loves

TRACEY STEVENS
& KATHERINE WUNDER, L.P.C.

AMAZING DREAMS
PUBLISHING
Asheville, North Carolina

Lesbian Sex Tips
A Guide for Anyone
Who Wants to Bring Pleasure
to the Woman She (or He) Loves

By Tracey Stevens & Katherine Wunder, L.P.C.

Published by:
Amazing Dreams Publishing
Post Office Box 1811
Asheville, NC 28802
orders@amazingdreamspublishing.com
http://www.amazingdreamspublishing.com

Unattributed quotations are by Tracey Stevens or Katherine Wunder.

Editing: Snowden Editorial Services

First Printing 2002

Printed in the United States of America

Library of Congress Control Number: 2002111005

ISBN: 0-9719628-2-0

This book is dedicated to the women and men who
think sex can be more than just procreating
and to all the ones who are brave enough
to seek help in understanding the
delicate nature of a woman's anatomy.

About the Authors

Tracey Stevens has written and illustrated stories since grade school. She won "The Daughters of the American Revolution Award" for writing an article on Southern slavery when she was eleven years old. In the early '90s she showed her anti-racism paintings throughout Florida, but since that time she has concentrated on writing. All her novels have themes of equality. A survivor of child abuse, she also

Tracey, left, and Kathy, right, sitting on their back porch in the Blue Ridge Mountains.

incorporates these issues in her writing, and says that her one mission in life is to bring the darkness of abuse into the light so that people who read her work will know that they are not alone. Tracey was the director of the Writers' Guild of Western North Carolina for two terms. She works as a graphic designer, and also in the fine arts field. She has a passion for horses, especially Spanish breeds, and credits her horse Shane for saving her from her childhood. She lives with her partner, Kathy Wunder, and a house full of animals.

Kathy Wunder grew up in various Southern states, but primarily Florida. In the '60s she and her parents lived in Natchez, Mississippi, and Kathy was greatly influenced by their work in the civil rights movement. She has been involved in the civil rights movement herself. After graduate school in Florida, Kathy joined Floridians United Against Discrimination. This group was fighting the American Family Association in their bid to make changes in the state constitution that would allow discrimination against the GLBT community. Her favorite pastimes include reading, going to movies, listening to music, cooking, and spending time with friends. She lives with Tracey; Phantom (her wolf-hybrid); Baby, Booger, Jessee, Cysco, W.T., Devon, Bilton, and Minky (the wild cats); Angelote De Luna (a Paso Fino stallion); and Mr. Pidge (Tracey's pigeon).

Disclaimer

This book is designed to provide information on loving women, with sections on women's basic physical anatomy; safer sex practices; sexually transmitted diseases; the importance of communication and the basic rules of how to communicate effectively; techniques on making love and sexual fulfillment of women; issues concerning sexual problems stemming from childhood sexual abuse; and the symptoms of domestic and partner abuse.

Because of the constantly changing information on some of these subjects, especially safer sex practices and facts on sexually transmitted diseases, you are urged to read other available material and learn as much as possible to protect yourself. The authors and Amazing Dreams Publishing shall have neither responsibility nor liability for any person or entity with respect to life choices or decisions made, directly or indirectly, from reading *Lesbian Sex Tips: A Guide for Anyone Who Wants to Bring Pleasure to the Woman She (or He) Loves.*

Every effort has been made to make this guide as accurate and complete as possible—at the last moment we updated it to include the much needed section on domestic partner abuse—however, there may be typographical errors or the information may have changed during the prepublication period. Therefore, this book should be used as a general guide, and not the ultimate authority on these subjects. For more information, see the bibliography/resource section in the back of this book.

Amazing Dreams Publishing is not just a company selling books—we are committed to forming a supportive community for lesbian, bi, transgendered, and "straight but not narrow" women. Visit our website for live links to resources including RAINN, which operates America's only national hotline for survivors of sexual assault. We have spent many hours researching the best places to find books, videos, and safer sex items and adult toys. We also offer free E-cards, designed by and for women, information on how to create your own art, and a future support chat room for women coming out. We invite you to visit us at:

www.amazingdreamspublishing.com

Contents

Acknowledgments

I would like to thank Rachel Blue Hudson, Robin Smith, and Susan Snowden, the goddesses of support and editing; Patricia Nell Warren, for wonderful counsel and much needed encouragement; Anne and Al Malatesta, my "adopted parents," who have been my most wonderfully supportive chosen family for many years; Craig Williamson, who urged me to begin this project and has been a much needed support throughout; my hot-blooded Spanish horse Shane, who still carries me through troubled times on his strong back; Angelote de Luna, the "pesky raffle colt" who is turning into an incredible stallion; the eight cats, large dog, and Mr. Pidge, who are the funniest housemates ever; Jack, James, and David, who are always "just a step away"; my "mother-in-outlaw," who has always treated me like another daughter; and Kathy, my partner and best friend, who not only helped me create this book, but has stood by me during the long lonely hours of writing my novels as well. To all the wonderful people who have encouraged my dreams, I am so blessed to have you in my life.

Tracey Stevens

To Tracey, my girlfriend and best friend, who encouraged me through my blocks in writing my chapters. For my mother, who has always been my "Rock of Gibraltar" and my first and longest guiding light, and the rest of my family, who have always loved and supported me no matter what. To my mentor and counselor, Pete Fisher, who was always teaching me and still does even though he is no longer with us. And to all the people who have ever touched my life, for helping me learn what I needed to, whether I wanted to or not, and helping me become the person I am today.

Kathy Wunder

Introduction

This how-to book is actually an excerpt from *How To Be A Happy Lesbian: A Coming Out Guide*. The reason I decided to turn part of *Happy Lesbian* into *Lesbian Sex Tips* is because I've had multitudes of discussions with all kinds of people who are dissatisfied with their sex lives. Many women complain that their partners just don't know what to do, and some of those women have very little knowledge of their own bodies and what it takes to please themselves. Not that I'm saying that everyone should go off and masturbate for days on end, but it does help to know thyself. The men who are having relationship troubles stemming from sex seem to truly want to make their partners happy, but most are too embarrassed to talk about it to anyone.

One such man I worked with several years ago. After he learned I was lesbian and that I didn't hate him for being male, we had some very meaningful talks. I spoke of life and prejudice and how hard it is to be different than most people, and he told me how difficult it is to be expected to always keep your emotions in and never cry. I wondered why he looked so sad, and after a few weeks he finally opened his heart to me. He was having trouble with his girlfriend, whom he was very much in love with, and said for some reason he just could not please her sexually. By the redness in his cheeks, I think it took a lot for him to admit this. I told him that there are many lesbians who don't know what to do either, and that he should not feel so bad about it. I suggested a couple of books, which he seemed squeamish about purchasing in a local book store. This was back before you could hop out on the Internet and buy whatever you wanted in relative anonymity. After several days he finally built up enough courage to ask me if I had any advice on what he could do to satisfy his girlfriend. He was not sexually harassing me in any way, which is why I agreed to reveal one lesbian sex tip. We both were embarrassed as I described what to do, but I told him because I cared about him and wanted to see him happy.

The next day his girlfriend came in the shop. She was smiling as she walked up to me, and with tears in her eyes she thanked me. Seems the sex tip had not only helped her to finally have an orgasm, but it had also provided a way for the two of them to start communicating like they never had before.

I don't know if they are still together, but I do know that that one little sex tip changed both their lives for the better. Their story is just one of the many which prompted me to put this manual together. It is written by me, someone who has been with women for more than half my life, and my partner who is a therapist. She taught me how to communicate, and believe me I don't get away with not discussing my feelings when I'm around her!

Sex is only a small part of who we really are, but being good at it is a wonderful gift to both you and your partner. If you truly want to become not only a better lover, but also a better human being, then open up your heart and communicate with the one that you love. Let go of society's BS that says we are supposed to automatically know how to please a woman because we are a lesbian, or because we are a man, or because we are whatever. Life is too short to go years longing for something better, so please talk about what you need. It may be one of the best things you could ever do for yourself and the person you love.

Tracey Stevens
Asheville, NC

Quotations From Women Who Love(d) Women

"The reward for conformity was that everyone
likes you except yourself."
—Rita Mae Brown, *Venus Envy*

"Creative minds have always been known
to survive any kind of bad training."
—Anna Freud

"I can stand out the war with any man."
—Florence Nightingale

"You must do the thing
which you think you cannot do."
—Eleanor Roosevelt

"It's pretty clear that the struggle
is to share the planet, rather than divide it."
—Alice Walker

"If you do not tell the truth about yourself
you cannot tell it about other people."
—Virginia Woolf

CHAPTER 1

Body talk and basic women's anatomy

What's the use of learning this?

Knowledge is power. If you apply yourself to learning everything you can about a woman's body, then you will have confidence in yourself and your abilities to bring your partner pleasure. If you know what a woman's sometimes subtle responses mean, then you can communicate on a deeper level and have a more satisfying relationship.

People ARE different.

The wonderful thing about being human is that we are all basically the same in structure, yet we are all incredibly different. What makes one person swoon in passion can make another totally disgusted. This is why both verbal and nonverbal communication are so important. In this chapter we will concentrate on basic anatomy and nonverbal, or bodily, communication. Verbal communication will be covered in Chapter 3.

What is bodily communication?

When you get cold, your skin may become covered with goose bumps and you can start to shiver. This is your body communicating, "Hey! It's freezing out here. Either get me a big coat, or let's go in by the fireplace." Your body is talking to you constantly, although many of these messages go unnoticed because they are such common occurrences. For most of us, sex does not happen twenty-four hours a day, which means that during arousal, our body's responses can be easily charted.

So what can a body say?

Pay attention to your own responses when you are beginning to get sexually aroused. What do you feel? Is it a heat wave that starts at your feet and burns through your center? Do you get flushed in the face, or red around your chest and neck? Does your heart start pounding and your respiration increase, or does your clitoris or penis swell up? Do your hands perspire or do chills break out over your back? Is your mind full of wonderfully intense images of what you would like to do with her?

These are just a few of the messages your body might whisper—or flat-out yell—when you are in the mood. The key is to be aware of your own messages, and then open yourself up to seeing your partner's.

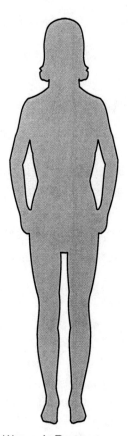

Women's Erogenous Zone (shaded in gray)

Erogenous zones—places that both give you the chills and make you hot

Many people think that erogenous zones are purely genital, but I've found this is far from true. When a woman is in the mood, her entire body can be an erogenous zone, and it's up to her partner to learn her favorite places. This can be done by paying close attention to what her body is telling you, or by her actually saying what she likes. Both ways are great, and should be used in conjunction with each other.

Breasts are more than "Got milk?"

Breasts come in all different shapes and sizes. Many women have petite soft mounds, while others have watermelon breasts that are about that solid. Some have huge nipples and some have tiny ones. It's pretty much all up to a woman's biology what she may have sitting atop her chest.

Some women's breasts are extremely sensitive to the touch, even to the point of producing orgasms, while others have boobs of steel, meaning no amount of wonderful stimulation will phase them.

Whatever you or your partner has, be proud of them. Even if a woman could wear her bra backwards and no one would notice, remember the old saying, "More than a mouthful is wasted."

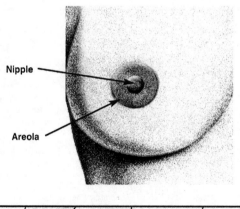

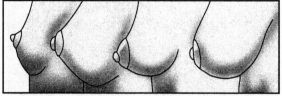

Different breast shapes

Introducing the vulva, and I don't mean the car.

Now we are going to get a little technical here, but this stuff is important, so I'll make it as entertaining as possible.

The vulva is composed of all the external parts of a woman's genitals. The whole thing is full of nerve endings, which makes it extremely sensitive to stimulation, so let's start from the outside in.

The Mound of Venus, or mons pubis, is that wonderfully soft pillow that sits atop a woman's pubic bone. It helps pad the area so if your partner is on top of you she won't get hurt. This area can be extremely sensitive in the beginning arousal state. It is usually covered with pubic hair shaped in an upside-down triangle which points the way to a woman's most magical place.

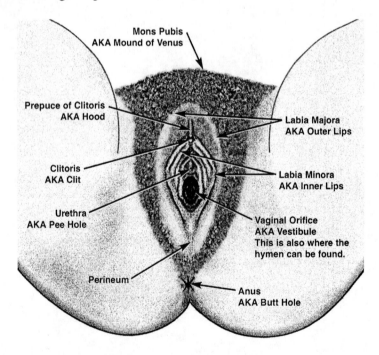

As you head down the path of the pointing triangle, you come to the labia majora, or large outer lips. This area consists of two folds of skin covered in hair, and it is also sensitive in the beginning stages of arousal. The outer labia is a great place to massage your lover by lightly rubbing the folds together. When you pull them apart, you will find the interior of the vulva.

The labia minora, or inner lips, have no pubic hair. The skin will be similar to your partner's mouth. This area is also a great place to massage (see Chapter 4 for an in-depth description). The two folds of the labia minora meet at the top and form the hood of the clitoris. Also called the prepuce, this skin covers the clitoris.

When stimulation occurs, the clitoris swells and becomes the size of a pea. This area is also known as "the little woman in the boat." The clitoris is the only organ in the whole world whose sole purpose is pleasure. There is nothing else like it in the entire animal kingdom. It is full of nerve endings, and, with the correct kind of stimulation, it can produce as many orgasms as a woman can take. It is sexual perfection at the highest degree and should be celebrated as much as possible.

The urethra, where urine passes through to the outside of the body, is the tiny hole located between the clitoris and the vaginal opening. To help prevent urinary tract infections, women should always wipe from front to back.

The vaginal orifice, or opening, is also where the hymen is located. The area around the opening, and an inch or so inside, is full of nerve endings. It is a wonderful place to tease your lover (more on that in Chapter 4). The vagina is a muscular, hollow tube which leads to the cervix. The cervix is the entrance to the uterus or womb. Tampons are inserted into the vagina, and babies leave the womb through the vagina.

Leading down to the anus is the perineum. This can be flat, slightly raised, or an actual ridge of skin, like a tiny labia minora. This small area is not that stimulating for most women I've known, although the skin around and in the anus is. The anus should be approached with caution. Some women love to have their anus rubbed; some enjoy penetration into the rectum; and some will totally freak out if you even mention going there. If you or your lover enjoy rectal probing activity, be sure to check out that section in Chapter 4.

CHAPTER 2

Plain talk about safer sex

What is "safer sex"?

Safer sex is a term used to let us know that no sex is the only safe sex. The term "safer sex" comes from the fact that no matter how cautious you are, accidents can happen and there is always a chance of becoming infected with an STD (sexually transmitted disease) when you are intimate with a partner. At this time one in five adults and one in four teenagers have been infected with an STD. Fortunately, there are all sorts of things you can do to help yourself stay healthy and to greatly decrease the possibility of being exposed.

But I thought women couldn't get STDs from each other.

If you think that, then you better cross your legs and pray, because it can happen. There have been cases reported which indicate that women have exposed each other to HIV (human immunodeficiency virus) as well as other types of STDs. Although the number of cases is much lower than other risk groups, it is still way better to be safe than sorry.

Women can be infected with STDs by the following: having unsafe sex with lesbians or with bisexuals who have been exposed through semen; sharing needles from IV drug use; piercing or tattooing without the proper sterilization techniques; having unsafe sex with men; or having unscreened artificial insemination and/or blood transfusions. Since 1985 blood and semen have been screened at most facilities. Many STDs are transmitted when blood, vaginal fluids (including menstruation), breast milk, or semen from an infected person enters your body or blood stream.

So what can I do to protect myself?

During the time when the acquired immune deficiency syndrome (AIDS) was running totally rampant in the United States, my stepdaughter came to me and asked, "What am I supposed to do, never have sex?" She was dating a new boyfriend she was serious about, and was upset by the media's constant bombardment saying the only way to be safe was to totally abstain from any sexual activity, period. Our little "lesbian family" had also known seventeen people who succumbed to complications of AIDS in six months' time, so we were all pretty paranoid. Because I wasn't in a high-risk group I really didn't know much more than she did, but I did know that STDs have been around probably as long as human beings have, and there are ways to protect yourself from getting them.

When considering intimacy in a new relationship, the first and most important thing is communication. I've known some straight women who were too embarrassed to ask the man they'd just picked up in a bar to wear a condom! I'd look at them and ask "You mean you are willing to get buck naked and screw like a wild dog in heat with a near stranger, but you can't talk about safer sex? Now how crazy is that?" They'd give me all kinds of excuses which essentially boiled down to the old idea that the man knows best. Well, I say that's pure B.S.! Let's not be ignorant and let other people decide our destiny. The great thing about being a woman today is that we don't have to play those kinds of games. When the issue of being together, really together, comes up, then it's up to one of you to bravely broach the subject of safer sex and who's done what.

Now I don't mean you need to rehash every moan you've ever made with lovers of the past, or dig up your most embarrassing sexual moment. But what I do mean is honestly look at your sexual histories and ask yourself and each other the following question: In the past five years have you or your partner, or ex-

> **Did you know?**
> In most states, there are laws against not telling your sexual partner if you know that you have a sexually transmitted disease such as HIV, AIDS, syphilis, or hepatitis B. Even if you used safer sex and no infection occurred, you can still be prosecuted for not revealing your status.

partners, participated in unsafe behaviors listed in the previous section? If so, you may want to have a general blood screening and an AIDS test. Wait 3-6 months after your last risky behavior and have a second test.

Since the virus HIV, which is thought to cause AIDS, can be lingering in your body long before showing up in your blood stream, it is a good idea to abstain from sex or use safer sex practices both six months before and after your AIDS test. Ask your health-care professional for the latest information on AIDS, and find out the best way to protect both you and your partner from a potentially deadly virus.

Handy items for safer sex

The way to be the most protected is to make sure that body fluids do not get inside your partner's body or get into her bloodstream via contact. Here are some barriers that will help you in this quest:

Latex gloves

These can be purchased at most drug or medical supply stores. They are essential to use if either partner has a cut or sore on the finger, hand, mouth, vagina, penis, or anus.

Using gloves can prevent the passage of a virus into your bloodstream. Some gloves come in designer colors; they can be powdered or non-powdered, and with or without water-based lubricating jellies. Make sure your fingernails are not jagged, which can snag and cut the latex. Gloves are great for all kinds of activities, from clitoral stimulation to vaginal or anal penetration. Make sure to change the gloves between vaginal and anal penetration. (See Chapter 4.)

Finger cots

These little roll-on mini condoms can be purchased at medical supply stores. They are good for clitoral stimulation and some vaginal or rectal penetration. Again, make sure your fingernails are not jagged. If your lover tends to "flood with love," meaning she gets wet enough to almost drown someone, then stick to the full latex gloves. They're much safer.

Dental dams

These five-inch square pieces of latex can be purchased at medical supply stores and come in several colors and flavors. Because unprotected cunnilingus (oral sex) is risky behavior, dental dams of some kind are essential. You can place the whole square over your partner's genitals. You can hold it yourself, or have your partner hold the top while you hold the bottom. Dental dams take a little practice to use safely. Mark the dam with an ink pen to make sure you don't use the wrong side if you happen to put it down, and throw away your dams after one use. If you tend to go out of your head when making love and feel you might not be able to keep track of a dental dam, then single-ply plastic wrap from the grocery store might be better for you. Used the same way as dental dams, plastic wrap can cover her like a big diaper, making wildness safer for everyone. Just make sure you get the non-porous plastic wrap. If it says microwavable on the box, that is the wrong kind. If you or your partner has trouble feeling stimulus through the barrier, then apply a water-based lubricant to the genital area beneath the dental dam.

Condoms

If you use dildos or dildo shaped vibrators, or you are with a man, then latex condoms are a good thing to have around. Instead of having

> **Did You Know?**
>
> Non-silicone vibrators and dildos have porous surfaces that can harbor bacteria or viruses. Even washing them with antibacterial soap may not disinfect them. For non-silicone toys, always use a fresh condom and clean them with antibacterial soap every time you use them for each partner. Silicone is safer because it is nonporous. You can boil a silicone dildo for 5 minutes in water, or wash it with antibacterial soap and hot water, and it will be safe to use without a condom.

to jump out of the bed to wash shared toys, just carefully peel off the used condom and slip on a new one. Make sure to pinch the air out of the end of the condom before rolling it on, because trapped air bubbles can cause a condom to break. You may also want to use a water-based lubricant to reduce friction, which can also cause breakage.

What's considered safe, risky, or unsafe behavior?

Some safe things you can do with your partner are hugging her tightly; massaging her everywhere but there; masturbation (sexually stimulating yourself) or watching her masturbate; phone sex; sharing fantasies; using vibrators or sex toys, but not sharing them without sterilizing them or changing the condom; dry kissing which means no tongue action; or tribadism, which means rubbing your bodies together without vaginal fluids, blood, semen, or breast milk exchanged.

Risky behaviors

Heavy French kissing can be risky, especially if you have a sore in your mouth or your gums bleed after brushing or flossing your teeth. Make sure to wait at least 30 minutes before kissing your partner if your gums are the bleeding type, and see a dentist. Bleeding gums can mean gum disease, which could lead to bone loss under your teeth, and you could lose your teeth over this condition.

Shared hand-to-genital contact with finger cots, gloves, or dental dams can be risky if a tear occurs in the latex. Oral sex while using a latex barrier can also be risky if the barrier moves or tears. Inserting your fist into your partner's vagina or rectum, known as fisting, while using a barrier or latex glove is always risky because of the pressure it puts on delicate vaginal or intestinal tissues, which are full of tiny blood vessels. Also, exchanging sex toys without washing them or using fresh condoms, any form of S&M or rough sex that involves piercing or shaving, or any sort of blood letting are very risky behaviors.

Unsafe behaviors

Some totally unsafe behaviors include: oral sex without a barrier, especially during menstruation; ingesting female fluids or ejaculate, or semen; sharing dildos or vibrators without a condom or without changing condoms in between users; licking the anal area, or rimming, without a dental dam or plastic wrap; fisting, especially without a glove; any kind of unprotected sex (not using a condom) with a man including oral, vaginal, or anal sex; sharing needles whether for drugs, piercing, or tattooing.

If you use IV drugs, DO NOT share your needles, syringes, or other equipment such as spoons or anything that a contaminated needle may come in contact with! This is very dangerous behavior because minute amounts of blood remain in used needles. In this vacuum state any virus can remain active much longer than when it has been exposed to air.

If you are compelled to use the same equipment for IV drug use, please sterilize it in the best way possible with bleach. Draw the bleach into the syringe through the needle and then shoot it into the sink. Do this twice. Rinse the entire syringe with uncontaminated water, fill with the water, and shoot through the needle several times to get all the bleach out.

If you and your partner are considering having a child

If you use a sperm bank, make sure that the donors are screened for all kinds of STDs, especially AIDS. If you use sperm donated by a male friend or your male partner, make sure he has had at least two negative HIV tests six months apart. The first test should be six months after his last possible exposure to HIV. The next test should be another six months later. In between the two tests and the date he supplies sperm, your donor, or male partner, must have no exposure whatsoever to HIV. This means he would have to be celibate or have been in a long-term, totally monogamous relationship with someone who is also not practicing any risky behaviors, such as IV drug use. At this time, the FDA is in the process of making it more difficult for gay men to donate sperm to sperm banks and to women they already know.

A serious warning

Just like drinking and driving can kill you or others, so can drug or alcohol use prior to or during sex. Your judgment can be impaired to the point of not using safer sex practices. Don't throw away what you've learned in this chapter and use the excuse of "I was too drunk to remember how to do it." Passion is a wonderful thing, but not quite wonderful enough to die for. Worldwide, millions of people have perished from STDs, especially AIDS. Please don't become one of the statistics.

A list of STDs, their symptoms, and general treatments

Chlamydia

Chlamydia is a bacterial disease and is the most common STD in the United States. Chlamydia is a dangerous disease to women because there are few or no symptoms. One to three weeks after exposure, a watery mucus discharge may or may not come from the vagina. There can also be a burning feeling during urination. Chlamydia can cause both pelvic inflammatory disease and sterility in women. It is usually treated successfully with antibiotics. In men, chlamydia can cause urethritis after one to three weeks' incubation. Symptoms of urethritis can include burning while urinating and/or a whitish or clear discharge.

Cold sores or fever blisters; clinical name - oral herpes or herpes 1

Cold sores, or fever blisters, are caused by the herpes virus. They can be transmitted by kissing, sharing washcloths or towels, or drinking from the same cup. After the first outbreak, the virus can be dormant for many years. It may reoccur if you are under stress, have a high fever, or are overexposed to the sun. Treatment is usually a prescription cream. Avoid spicy or acidic foods, which may aggravate the condition.

Crabs or cooties; clinical name - pubic lice

Pubic lice are tiny crab-like insects that take up residence in the genital region. The most common symptoms are intense itching caused from their bites, and small dark spots of crab feces left in your underwear. These nasty little critters can be spread by having sex with an infected partner or by coming in contact with contaminated clothing, bedding, or toilet seats. Wash in hot water or dry clean all bedding and clothing that has come in contact with the lice. Treatment is fairly simple with over-the-counter medication.

Genital herpes or herpes 2; clinical name - herpes simplex

Genital herpes is an incurable viral infection. It is spread by sex, and occasionally by fingers that have herpes blisters or sores. Nearly 70 percent of herpes is transmitted through asymptomatic shedding, which means the person infected has no outward symptoms but may still spread the virus. Studies show that at this time almost one-third of sexually active, unmarried adults have herpes. The most common symptoms appear two to ten days after infection and can include swollen glands, a general run-down feeling or flu-like symptoms, and an itching or burning pain in the genital area. Small red bumps will form that can turn into white, blistery-looking sores. These sores usually appear on the vaginal lips of women, but may also affect the cervix or anal area. In men, the blisters occur most commonly on the penis, but they can also appear on the urethra or rectum.

The initial symptoms of genital herpes last about three weeks. These symptoms may return and are sometimes caused by stress, but will heal much faster than the onset of the disease. It is most contagious when the symptoms are present, but it can be spread at other times as well. Herpes can cause miscarriage of a pregnancy, and it can be passed on to newborns or cause serious health consequences if open sores are present during childbirth. In these cases a cesarean section will often be performed. Safer sex practices should always be used if one of the partners has herpes. Treatment for the disease is usually a prescription of an oral antiviral medication. It is important to keep the sores clean by daily washing with soap and water and then carefully drying them.

Genital warts caused by the human papilloma virus (HPV)

Genital warts are caused by a viral infection and are spread through vaginal, anal, and oral intercourse and during childbirth. The most common symptoms are small, reddish, round, possibly itchy bumps which can be throughout the genital or anal areas, or in the throat. In women, genital warts usually appear on the labia, the opening and inner third of the vagina, and the cervix. Common locations for men are just inside the opening of the urethra, on the head or the coronal ridge of the penis, or on the inner surface of the foreskin. These warts can range in size from tiny solitary growths to large masses. If allowed to grow, the warts can even block openings of the vagina, anus, or throat. Some strains of this virus may increase the risk of cervical cancer in women. Treatments include chemical or surgical removal, prescription creams, or freezing with liquid nitrogen. Even if genital warts are removed, the virus that causes them is still in the body, which can cause future outbreaks.

Gonorrhea

Gonorrhea is caused by the bacterium *Neisseria gonorrhoea*. It is the oldest known STD, and was mentioned in the writings of Plato. There are few or no symptoms in most women infected, making it a very dangerous disease to both women and their partners. If symptoms do occur they are usually within two to ten days after infection and include having a thick, yellowish discharge from the vagina, burning pain when urinating, pelvic inflammation, swelling of the vulva, and possibly arthritic-like pain in the shoulder. In later stages this disease can cause bleeding between periods. Most men develop a yellowish discharge and have painful, frequent urination. Ten percent of men who have gonorrhea may not show any symptoms at all, which means that they can pass on the disease without realizing it. Gonorrhea can be spread through any unprotected sexual activity. If left untreated, it may move into your joints resulting in arthritis, cause problems with your heart or central nervous system, or cause pelvic inflammatory disease in women. It can also blind newborn babies. Treatments for gonorrhea include antibiotics and pain relievers.

Hepatitis B

Hepatitis B is a highly contagious virus spread by unprotected sex, intimate contact such as kissing or using the same toothbrush, and needle-sharing. Nearly one hundred times more infectious than HIV, hepatitis B is the the only sexually transmitted disease that has a vaccine. It seldom has symptoms during the most contagious stages, though symptoms may develop such as fever, nausea or vomiting, fatigue, and loss of appetite. It can cause severe liver damage resulting in death if not diagnosed. No medical cure exists for hepatitis B. It is advisable to stop all drinking of alcohol, stay home and rest if you feel tired, and drink at least eight glasses of water a day.

HIV; clinical name - human immunodeficiency virus

HIV is a virus which may change to the acquired immune deficiency syndrome (AIDS). First diagnosed in 1981,

AIDS has become a disease of epidemic proportions, so far killing an estimated twenty million people worldwide. Linked to infections caused by the human immunodeficiency virus (HIV), AIDS is most commonly spread by sexual contact or IV drug use. It is not caused by casual contact such as shaking hands, hugging, or even drinking out of the same glass.

HIV infection can go undetected for years with few or no symptoms. HIV destroys the infection-fighting white blood cells, gradually wearing down the body until any small cold that is regularly fought off could be almost life-threatening. When the immune system collapses, opportunistic infections develop. Symptoms can be one or several of the following: fatigue or a general sick feeling; fevers, chills and/or night sweats; swollen lymph glands in the back of the neck or armpits; frequent long-lasting colds; weight loss; diarrhea caused by no apparent reason; coughing and general breathing problems; sores that are hard to heal, or the purple lesions called Kaposi's sarcomas.

As of yet, there is no vaccine against AIDS, and the safest sex possible is an absolute must for anyone diagnosed with the disease. There are several treatments available to stabilize a person with symptoms, but at this time no cure is available.

As I said at the beginning of this chapter, AIDS wiped out seventeen of my friends in six months' time, and they were not all gay men either. In other countries AIDS has been primarily a heterosexual disease. I consider it a horrible plague which was not taken seriously by the U.S. government for many years. I'm not sure if the reason was because it was first considered a "homosexual disease" but the bottom line is this: because AIDS was left unchecked in the United States it has spread into all populations. But remember, just because you are carrying the HIV virus does not mean that it will convert to AIDS.

I have known people who have lived with HIV for fifteen years and more. What they say is this: "The best thing to do is to take very good care of yourself, including proper diet, and exercise. You must alleviate all forms of drugs, including drinking and smoking—essentially anything that will wear your immune system down. Make sure to get the right amount of rest, do not over-work or over-stress yourself, and do not constantly dwell on your disease." The last statement, I believe, is one of the most important. If you keep thinking you are going to get sick, your body will follow what your mind is saying, and I know this for a fact.

I had an acquaintance who seemed perfectly healthy. Her sister was a hospice nurse in another state who worked primarily with AIDS-related illnesses. One of her clients turned out to be my friend's ex-boyfriend. Her sister called and told her that her ex was dying of AIDS and that she had better get tested. This was six years after their breakup. My friend had the test and turned out to be positive, and within a few months she was gone from this earth. Her husband, with whom she'd been having unprotected sex for several years, has had many tests since her death, but has never tested positive.

I'm not saying it is better not to know if you are infected with HIV or not, especially if you could risk giving the disease to someone you love. What I am saying is that a positive mental outlook can go a long way in keeping you healthy, not just in the case of AIDS, but in your whole life.

Molluscum contagiosum

Molluscum contagiosum is a fairly harmless infection of the genital area or thighs. Caused by a virus, the symptoms are small, pinkish-white lumps that if squeezed may express a cheesy material. The infection is spread by intimate contact and/or sexual intercourse. It usually will disappear on its own within three to twelve months, or your dermatologist can remove the lumps by freezing, chemicals, or electrical current.

Pelvic inflammatory disease (PID)

Pelvic inflammatory disease is a reproductive system infection in women that may be caused from other STDs such as gonorrhea or chlamydia. Symptoms can include nausea, chills, fever, vomiting, abdominal pain, spotting between periods, and heavy bleeding or blood clots during menstruation. If left untreated, PID can cause sterility in women. The best treatment is a combination of antibiotics and rest, with no sexual activities.

Syphilis

Syphilis is one of the oldest known STDs and was first seen in fifteenth century Europe. Syphilis is caused by an organism called *Treponema pallidum* and can be passed by kissing and other forms of sexual contact. Syphilis can cause brain damage, and nervous system and heart failure. Symptoms begin ten days to three months after infection and include painless sores that appear on or in the mouth, rectum, or genitals. These sores are called chancre, which is pronounced "shanker." Chancres usually begin as a small red spot which develops into a pimple. The pimple will ulcerate, forming a sore that is usually surrounded by a red rim. Chancres usually heal in four to six weeks, which makes people who are infected believe that the problem has cured itself. Second stage syphilis can begin anywhere from one week to six months after the chancre heals. The symptoms include a pale red rash which often begins on the palms of the hands or soles of the feet, fever, sore throat, rash, joint pains, and patchy hair loss. Highly contagious sores may also form around the genitals or anus. In the third stage, syphilis attacks the nervous system and can destroy bone and joints and can even lower the blood supply to the brain. Treatment is only effective during the first, second, and symptomless stages and usually involves antibiotics, such as long-acting forms of penicillin.

Trich; clinical name - trichomoniasis

Trichomoniasis is a vaginal infection caused by a parasite. Symptoms begin four to twenty days after exposure and include yellowy-green vaginal discharge with an odor, pain during sex, or painful urination. Treatments include antibiotics and abstaining from sex. Even if one partner is not showing overt symptoms, both should be treated at the same time to prevent reinfection.

Yeast infection or thrush; clinical name - candidiasis

A common yeast infection is caused by the fungus *Candida*. *Candida* is usually present in the mouths, intestines, and vaginas of most healthy women. When the body's acidity changes an overgrowth of candida can cause a yeast infection. Symptoms can include a dry itchy feeling around the vulva; a thick, cottage cheese-like discharge from the vagina that may or may not have a strong odor. A yeast infection can be spread through sex, including oral sex. This fungus can also affect the throat, tongue, or lining of the mouth and is then known as thrush. Thrush can

21

develop in both men and women. The best treatments are prescription or over-the-counter antifungal creams or suppositories.

For more info

If you think you may have been exposed to an STD, see a doctor or go to a health clinic. You can also contact the National STD/AIDS Hotline at 1-800-227-8922.

The most important thing about STDs is not to be exposed to them. The only way to do this is to be safe and communicate openly with your partner. If you have trouble with communication, be sure to read the next chapter. It was written by the "Goddess of Communication," my counselor girlfriend, Kathy. She's taught me more about verbal communication than anyone else, which is why I've asked her to write the chapter.

CHAPTER 3

Communication:
The key to working relationships

Communication—seems easy—but is it really? The romantic *ideal* is that your partner knows just what to say and knows what you want and need, and you won't have to say a thing. We get this message from movies, TV, and romance novels. The reality is that no one can read our minds, and we can't get mad at our partners if they don't give that hug when we need it, or say "I love you" when we want to hear it the most.

The hard part is learning to ask for that hug or those three little words that mean so much. Waiting for your partner to say or do something you want, and her not knowing it, causes hard feelings on your part and leaves your loved one wondering what's wrong. It may even get to the point where you give her the silent treatment or become irritable. More than likely, your partner will then get upset and a fight will start. At some point she may have even asked you what was wrong and you may have answered "nothing."

This chapter will help you learn how to communicate more effectively so that the above scenario happens less and smoother communication happens more often.

We all have heard that there are two types of communication: verbal and nonverbal. You never have one without the other. What might be surprising is that nonverbal takes up the largest percentage of communication with verbal coming in a distant second.

The reason for this is that the words are only a small part of communication. The bulk comes from facial expressions and body language. For instance, suppose you run into a friend and ask him how he is doing. He openly smiles and says, "Fine." His arms are at his sides and they're relaxed. Now you run into another friend and ask the same question. This person smiles tightly, nothing more than a showing of her teeth; her eyebrows are pulled down; her arms are crossed over her chest, and in an angry tone of voice she replies, "Fine!" Would you think your friend was "fine" or would you think the answer was not matching all the other cues given?

We process the nonverbals so automatically we usually don't think about them, we just react to them. There are also those times when we may ask someone how they are and they say "fine" but they seem subdued. Again, a nonverbal and more subtle cue than the circumstance just described, but no less meaningful.

In the circumstance where the verbals don't match the angry nonverbals one would usually ask, "What's wrong?" In the circumstance where the messages don't match and are subtle, we may choose to ask if everything really is all right, or we may leave it alone and take it at face value. The best option here would be to err on the side of caution and ask anyway.

Remember: pay close attention to the verbals and pay even closer attention to the nonverbals.

Basic rules of communication

None of us really learns to communicate effectively. Most of us have poor role models in our parents and other relatives, on TV, and in movies or books. This is a general statement but it applies to many people. We have learned to blame other people for what we feel, and we are taught to put the responsibility on them instead of on us where it belongs.

How often have you heard, or made, these statements? "You made me mad." "You made me feel like an idiot." "You embarrassed me." "You made me happy." Or "You made me excited." The reality is no one can "make" us feel anything without our permission. Our reactions are our own and we react to circumstances or others.

Think of a time when you were driving some place you really didn't want to go, to do something you really didn't want to do. Say someone cut you off in traffic and you got mad. You may have cussed and yelled at the other person through your windshield, shot a bird, or passed and given the other driver a nasty look as you sped by. Now think of a time when a similar circumstance happened and you were in a good mood and looking forward to getting to your destination. Someone cut you off and you just shrugged your shoulders, or maybe you cursed the person under your breath, but you decided you were in too good of a mood to let something so trivial get under your skin; then you focused back on looking forward to getting where you were going.

This is an example of how we are in control and not someone else. It shows how we react to circumstances and how they don't control us. This is the basis of good communication for anyone—accepting responsibility for your feelings.

The following are other basic ground rules to help you and your partner, or you and anyone else, to communicate more effectively. Following them can stop arguments from turning into fights, or stop misunderstandings from becoming arguments.

Them's fightin' words!

The basic rules of communication are as follows:

1. Don't use the words "should," "would," "could," "never," or "always." These are all words that are guaranteed to raise the hackles of another person, and the automatic response to one of them is to feel the

need to defend oneself with an angry retort. If you really want to make it a *coup de grace*, point your finger while saying, "You never . . ." or "You should . . ." or use one of the other fightin' words. Those two things together will really push someone into overdrive and a full-scale war could ensue. Another fightin' word to never use is "why?" I learned this the hard way. While I was working on my master's degree one of my instructors had warned us not to use that word too frequently when working with clients. I decided to experiment and asked a client "why" a number of times. Talk about a reaction. People usually respond in an angry manner when asked this because they feel that they are being challenged, not believed, or that their integrity is being questioned. That little experiment was over ten years ago, and I have never repeated it.

2. Don't get into a shouting match. Keep your voice neutral and nonaccusatory. Use a conversational tone and make declarative statements that allow you to take responsibility for your own feelings. Examples of this would be "When you said such-n-such I felt so-n-so." Or "When you did such-n-such, I felt so-n-so." This enables you to take the responsibility for your reaction to the situation without your partner feeling that there is something she needs to defend.

3. Avoid using "but" and "yeah, but." How many times have you either said or heard someone else say something like, "I know I shouldn't say that but . . ."? What this really means is you don't really mean what comes before the "but." Your real intention is what comes after the "but." When someone says "yeah, but" it has the same hidden meaning. For example,

someone gives you some advice you asked for. Your response is "Yeah, but I just can't do that." You have just dismissed the advice you asked for and have given an excuse as to why you don't want to follow that advice. Also remember that when you say "can't" it really means "won't." If someone were to ask you if you could go to the store for them right now and you're busy, you may say, "I can't right now. Maybe later." The true meaning is that you are choosing to follow through with what you are planning, or doing, and so you won't go until later.

4. Agree on your rules for discussion before you ever have your first argument, and agree to stick with the rules. Keep in mind that if the two of you can't agree on something, you may be better off agreeing to disagree on a subject. One of the rules that goes with those listed in this section is to agree that if your voice or your partner's voice becomes angry, or if you both begin to shout or become overly emotional or blaming, then it is time to stop and take a break. This means that if you reach this point, one of you should go to one room and the other one to a different room. One person can go for a walk while the other soaks in a tub. Anything to separate from each other until everyone has cooled off and both parties are willing to meet back at the discussion table in a calm manner. One of you may notice before the other that things are escalating, so work out a word, phrase or a hand sign to indicate the need for a time out. One of you can use it when needed in the heat of an argument.

5. DO NOT EVER ARGUE IN BED OR GO TO BED IN AN ARGUMENT. If you argue in bed then you can

start equating bed with the place to fight, not with the place of love, safety, and security that it needs to be. If an argument starts in bed, get up and go to another room to have that argument.

6. Allow each person to have time to express feelings without interruption. If someone doesn't get to complete a statement and is frequently interrupted, she may get more and more frustrated and begin to feel that what she says doesn't matter.

7. The discussion needs to be kept only to the issue that is the problem. Don't bring up things that happened two weeks, two months, two years, or two decades ago. The issue must be kept to the one that is affecting you and your partner right now. Don't turn it into every issue that you have ever had in your relationship.

8. Choose a time and place to bring up an issue if you are unable to discuss it at the time it occurs, and commit to it. Come to the table with all of your concentration on ways to clear up the problem, and work on leaving chips off your shoulder.

9. Work with your partner to find solid, and if need be, creative solutions to your problem. This may involve alternatives and compromises for both of you. An example may be that if everything turns into an argument then go someplace public to discuss the issue. Or go outside on the lawn to have that argument. The idea here is to put yourselves into a place where neither of you will be raising your voice or escalating.

10. Always start out by giving the other person a

positive, or something you really appreciate that your partner has done. After this is stated, move onto the statements of behaviors that are at issue. Then end with a positive. In other words start with a positive, place the issue in the middle, then end it with a positive. This allows your partner to feel that you are not always picking out bad things about her, and it also allows you to focus on the positive things about your partner.

11. Do not target your partner's sensitive areas. In other words, don't target her with things that you know are going to get her angry and upset. For instance, if she doesn't like the way her mother does something, don't tell her, "You're just like your mother. You take cheap shots the way she does."

12. After you get things resolved to a comfortable place for both of you, make a point to check in with each other to discuss how things are going. You can schedule this or do it on an impromptu basis. Checking in with each other allows you and your partner to fine-tune progress and changes.

13. If you and your partner argue, apologize if you are wrong. Don't give any excuses with your apology. When you do this, it comes across as not taking responsibility for your emotional reaction, not only to your partner, but to yourself as well.

The point of all these rules is to help both you and your partner have a win/win outcome and not a winner/loser result. If you find you have a winner/loser result then someone will feel taken advantage of. If this happens too many times, then hard feelings start to develop.

Arguments are not a bad thing and are not to be avoided at all costs. They are where growth comes from, and a healthy form of communication that can also enhance your relationship.

Coming out

Coming out to others is a personal decision. We have the right to tell those we choose that we're lesbian or bisexual. By the same token, we do not have the right to tell others that someone else is gay, lesbian, or bisexual. Coming out is an intensely personal experience so a good rule of thumb is, I mind my business and you mind yours.

Each of us must choose if we wish to be in or out of our own personal closets, and to what degree. Some are out to friends and no one else; some are out to friends and family, but not at work; and some are out in all circumstances. It is up to the individual to decide what is right for her.

You have to decide how comfortable you are with coming out, and with whom you wish to be out. Do some research on the topic by reading books specifically about the coming out process, and decide what suits you best and what course you wish to follow. There are also books on coming out to your parents (see the bibliography and resource section). If you choose to come out to your parents, it may be helpful to have a book for them in one hand and information on PFLAG (Parents and Friends of Lesbians and Gays) in the other.

PFLAG is a national organization with chapters in cities all over the United States. Their primary function is to serve as a support group for people who have lesbian, gay, or bisexual family and/or friends. There are also lesbians and gays who are members of these groups.

Trust

Trust is the most important thing in a relationship. If you don't have trust, you don't really have a relationship. There are a lot of couples who stay very insular in a bid to protect their relationship. In the long run this does more damage than good. Some couples also give up individual interests and only do things together. This is usually done because there is not always respect for relationships by other people.

The point here is that you may run into situations where someone else is approaching you, or your partner, and expressing a sexual interest. This is where the trust comes in. If it's you, just handle it in a calm and firm manner. Let the other person know that you are in a committed relationship, and that you are not interested. If someone is flirting with your partner, or your partner tells you that someone has approached her, let her handle the situation. If you love and trust her, then you need to allow her to handle the situation. In the case where a partner is having an affair, or has had an affair, you must remember that this is a symptom of a problem in your relationship. The goal is to work with your partner if you are having problems by communicating what your issues are in the relationship and the two of you working on the issues. If this doesn't resolve anything, then I suggest that you get outside help by getting into couples counseling. (See Chapter 5.)

Remember, some people have concerns about going to a therapist and feel that there is a social stigma associated with seeking professional help. Therapy doesn't mean that you or your partner, or both of you, are crazy. It simply means that sometimes we need someone who is outside the situation to help us see things more clearly.

Relationship problems are like getting lost driving to

somewhere you've never been or only been once or twice before. Someone gave you directions but you left the second page at home. So you stop and ask directions from someone who knows the area because you do remember the street name and address of where you are going. A good therapist is the person you stop and ask for directions.

How to discuss sexually transmitted diseases

There may be a lower incidence of sexually transmitted diseases in certain populations than in others, but that doesn't mean that this should not be discussed, especially if one of you does have a sexually transmitted disease. In most states, you are required by law to tell a potential sexual partner if you have a sexually transmitted disease. Even if no infection occurs and you are using safer sex, you can still be prosecuted. In some states this is considered a felony offense.

It can be very uncomfortable broaching the subject of STDs with someone you are interested in. Gauging the time to do this is the hard part. Obviously, you want to do this prior to being intimate with the other person and not after. This conversation is to protect both you and your potential partner. You need to check with the other person regarding high-risk sexual behaviors she (or he) may have had in the past with other people, and you need to share the same information. You'll also need to discuss safer sex practices and getting tested for HIV and hepatitis B if you feel it is necessary. If the test results come back negative on both of you, you can ask your health-care professional when it would be OK to have unprotected sex, unless you both have agreed to have an open relationship. Then you get to discuss a whole new topic— how to handle that situation.

It may be uncomfortable to broach the subject with a new

partner about STDs, safer sex, and past risky sexual behavior, but the possible end result if you don't could be contracting a fatal or serious illness. Truth be told, there is no good time to bring this up and discuss this topic. The best thing to do is to just jump in and start asking questions after prefacing them with something like, "I'm not sure how to bring this up, but I would like to discuss something important with you to protect us both . . ." If you are not comfortable with this statement, find something that you are comfortable with and use it to open up the discussion. Sometimes it is hard to judge when you should broach the subject. You are the best judge of when to talk about sexual matters and concerns, as you can sense when the two of you are moving to that place of increased sexual attraction.

Pillow talk

One of the hard things about a new relationship for some is the difficulty in telling your partner what you do and do not want sexually. There may be something that is really a turn-off for you. If you are uncomfortable with asking your partner to do or say certain things during sex, have a discussion outside the bedroom and at a neutral time. The goal here is to reach the point, if you're not there already, to be able to openly say exactly what you want and how you want it while you are together in bed. And make sure to use basic rules of communication discussed earlier in this chapter.

Let your partner know that this is what you want to talk about, and open the discussion in a calm and clear manner. It may even help you to plan out what you want to cover prior to your talk. Let her know what the issue(s) is(are) and what makes you comfortable, and ask her what she wants. Work on points of compromise as long as you feel that you can compromise over whatever the concern or issue is.

In summary, be open, honest, and compassionate when discussing issues or concerns with your partner and follow the rules contained in this chapter. It won't stop you from arguing, but hopefully it will stop you from fighting, and give you two an opportunity to communicate openly and honestly, and to learn about yourself and each other.

CHAPTER 4

Romance and the art of making lesbian love

As I said before, I have met many people who have never had a satisfying sex life. Lots of straight women don't feel anything during sex, because their partners don't realize that jumping on and humping till the cows fly up your butt just doesn't get it for everyone.

According to a report done by Kinsey, lesbian women are far more likely to have orgasms than straight women. One of the reasons for this is because lesbians enjoy bringing their partners to arousal and most times this is done in a very slow and deliberate way. It is not a "fast feel of the boobs and on to the pleasure tunnel," which is usually a quick satisfaction for straight men only. Most lesbians also know that making love can encompass more body parts than just your genitals.

I met one couple who were both miserable because the husband had become impotent. He couldn't take Viagra because of health issues, and the two of them were ready to break up over it. After this story, where the wife was near tears and the husband was embarrassed, I just looked at them for a few moments, deciding if they could take what I was about to say and not faint or go into cardiac arrest, and then I just blurted out "Hey, I don't have a penis and I can give my girlfriend as many orgasms as she can stand!" As I waggled my ten fingers at them, they looked at me like I was nuts. I gave them a pretty explicit lesbian porno movie, complete with sex toys and vibrators, and sent them home to figure it out for themselves. I guess they did because they seemed way happier after that, and they didn't break up.

The point I'm making here for the guys is that your penis

is kind of like a woman's clitoris. If you don't stimulate it, an orgasm might not happen. Like it or not, some women can not come from just penetration, so you may want to learn some other techniques so that the woman you love is truly satisfied. You can then hold your head up high because your new name could be "Mr. Stud Muffin" instead of "Lame old non-caring weasel in the sack."

Now I'm not blaming just the guys for the plight of human sexual dysfunction. I've also met women who know nothing abut their own bodies and have never masturbated or had an orgasm. I know this for a fact, because I've been with two such women myself.

My first partner had never been with anyone, and she knew nothing about masturbation. We brought each other out at sixteen. My second partner had been married to a man for a while, and then was with a woman for seven years. She'd been with two people for extended periods of time and had no idea about what a clitoris or a G-spot was. She'd never had an orgasm in her entire life! I thought I could certainly remedy that, but for the longest time she would not allow me to give her a clitoral orgasm. She just could not handle the intense feelings of arousal. After a year together, and with her permission, I finally preformed a few lesbian sex tips, and, believe me, the house practically rocked when she reached orgasm. She was amazed and a whole lot happier being totally satisfied inside and out. The sad part to me was that out of all those years she was in long-term relationships, no one cared enough to show her how to really make love. Or maybe they didn't know how to do it themselves.

This is where we are lacking as human beings today. Society lays this crap on men's doorstep, that they are supposed to automatically know how to please a woman, and women are told that it is awful to touch themselves. How can anybody know anything if no one talks about it, or just says that they are enjoying sex when they are really hating it. It's not good for the man and it sure isn't good for the women. It is just screwed up.

So with that said, I will get off my dyke soapbox for now and write some information for anyone who wants to know more about a woman's body. If you don't know what areola, mons pubis, prepuce, or labia majora mean then you may want to go back and review Chapter 1. I will be using these very important words to explain how to give your partner an orgasm, and it would be good for you to know what I am talking about. There are many ways to make love to a woman, but I just list some basic techniques that I know work for sure. It's up to you to develop your own style, and this explicit step-by-step chapter will help get you started.

Romance, the best way to keep a relationship happy

Romance means different things to different people. Some view being romantic as having dinner ready for their partner the minute she walks in from work, or cleaning the house and washing her clothes. Others view it as candy and kisses, or flowers and dinner dates. The important thing to find in any relationship is what each partner considers romantic, and work towards meeting each other's dreams. This is one way to keep the relationship going for many years, but it's a hard thing to know without asking.

My girlfriend and I just figured this out a few months back, and we've been together for nine years! All this time I was fixing her dinner and doing things that I thought were romantic, only to find out that she was missing romance because her definition was way different than mine. This comes back to the old communication issue that can get neatly swept under the rug because of the business of being alive and making a living. Many of us tend to get caught up in the responsibilities of life, and forget to take time for the fun of it.

Talk to your partner and find out what being romantic means to her. It might come down to just a few words, like "Make wild love to me on a bed of rose petals," or doing something special like cleaning out the cat box and sweeping the floor. Whatever it is, see if you can make her dreams come true. Maybe she will do the same for you.

Some romantic things to do

Have flowers sent to her at work; send fun cards on all holidays, or when she's feeling blue. These can also be cards you make or even e-mail cards—anything that says you care. Cook her a lovely dinner, using your best plates, even if they are plastic, and maybe use cloth napkins if you have them; turn the lights low and eat by candlelight. If you can't cook, fake it. Buy take-out and put it on plates like you fixed it yourself. Buy snuggly flannel sheets for your bed in the winter, and cool satin ones for the summer. Leave her favorite candy on her pillow, or let her sleep late and serve her breakfast in bed. Tell her how gorgeous she is and how much she means to you whenever you think about it. Give each other romantic body massages, or wonderful foot and hand massages while you are sitting around watching TV.

Encourage and support each other's dreams and goals. Let each other go and do things on your own—not everyone has the same hobbies. Make her something special, or fix something up you find at a garage sale. Have a night each week when you do things together, like have dinner at a nice restaurant or go on a date to see a romantic movie. Play and laugh together. Have deep, long, soul-talks in bed, and make sure to argue somewhere else. Plan short vacation getaways as often as you can afford to. Find fun free things to do, like take the dog for walks at a beautiful place you discover, or drive out in the country to somewhere you've never been. Bring home a funny movie if one of you is sad or depressed. And always, always concentrate on each other's positive qualities.

These are just a few of the things you can do to be romantic. Think of what you would like, and if it seems like your partner would enjoy it, do it for her, but remember we are all different. Make sure to always ask each other what could change to make your relationship better.

First things first

There are as many ways to make love as there are ways to be romantic, so what I'm going to concentrate on are basic techniques that will assure that you can satisfy a woman.

First off, if you are not absolutely positive that either of you has not been exposed to a sexually transmitted disease, make sure you practice safer sex. If you skipped Chapter 2 now would be a good time to read it. I cannot stress how important it is for you to study that chapter. How to have safer sex could save your life, and the descriptions of the diseases and what they can do to you if you catch them should prompt you to never take a risk.

I wrote that chapter so you would be aware of the danger that is out there secretly waiting for the person who thinks "It won't ever happen to me." It scared me when I was doing the research, because when I was young safer sex for lesbians was never discussed. The diseases were out there just the same, and I'm real happy I didn't catch any of them.

I don't want you to catch any of them either. As I said before, I had seventeen friends die of AIDS in one year, and that has had a lasting effect on me. I also have three friends who have hepatitis B, two who have genital herpes, and one who has genital warts. Don't let yourself become a statistic. Read the scary Chapter 2 so that you will never take any chances with your life.

Before foreplay—what to do to get her, and you, in the mood

This is the thing that many people forget, or simply don't understand. Making love with a woman starts in the head and moves south, not the other way around. If you walk up and grab a woman's crotch, she might slap the crap out of you, so don't do that unless you are play fighting and it is a known fact that she is OK with that behavior.

Everyone is different. I had one girlfriend who got aroused by going to the fair, and I knew someone else who would get so turned on in the vegetable section of the grocery store that she would have to leave or face having a spontaneous orgasm next to the cukes. You never know what is going to put someone in the mood, which leads back to communication, but here are a few ideas to begin with:

Take her to a nice restaurant and during dinner rub your foot up her leg under the table cloth–make sure you are not wearing army boots or shoes with sharp buckles when you do this. While watching a romantic movie, rub the palm of her hand in the darkness of the theatre, then move up her arm to her breasts. Walk up behind her while she is making lunch and move your chest across her back while gently kissing her neck. Spontaneous slow dancing in the living room while listening to some favorite music is always nice.

While driving reach over and rub her arm, just barely skimming her breast. Massage her back and then ask to massage her front. Kiss her hands, beginning with the back then going for the palm and her fingers, possibly sucking them into your mouth–don't chew on them like your pet bulldog chews his rawhide treats though. While standing, kiss her passionately and gently press your body into hers.

These are just a few of the basic things that can start to turn someone on. Be the detective, find out what it is that she really wants, and then determine if you can do it.

Do not be afraid of being a great lover

When I was first discovering who I was, I read a book about lesbians' fantasies. The woman who wrote it was French and she gave some advice that I never forgot—do not be afraid to do anything to please the woman you love. Now, I don't think she meant you should go beyond your boundaries and hang upside down whipping yourself with a horse crop until you resemble a red-butted baboon, but what I do think she meant was don't limit yourself to what you think you can do. Be open to new experiences, and you will become a great lover.

That brings up another point, which is different in every situation. It is usually better to go slowly and take your time when making love to a woman, but some people don't like it that way. You have to be responsive to what your partner wants in order to fulfill her needs and yours. She may go through times when she wants slow, passionate love, or other times she may ask you to take her on her knees from behind like a dog. You just have to be open enough and brave enough to give up any ego you have about how great you are in bed, and go where she needs you to go and do what she needs you to do. You also need to know your own limitations and be able to openly discuss these when they come up, which goes back to that chapter on communication.

Another important part of making love is cleanliness. Unless your partner likes how you look and smell after mowing your lawn in August, make sure you are as clean as possible. This includes your hair; your hands and fingernails—make sure they are trimmed short, or filed so that there are no rough edges; and most importantly your genitals—no one likes a rolled toilet paper strand as an appetizer, so scrub up! If you tend to have a strong, wild odor about you, then you might want to take a sudsy bath either with or without your partner before making love. This advice goes for both men and women. I've had several bisexual friends tell me that the only time they smell like a fish is after they've had unprotected sex with a man who had an unclean penis. They never have that odor when they are with women. So men, listen up. If you don't want to be chewing on a tuna casserole then wash that thing, and always wear a condom to protect yourself if you don't know for sure that your partner has not been exposed to an STD. It could save your life.

So how do I know when she's getting in the mood?

Most people can't read each other's minds, so you can either ask your partner if she is getting turned on by what you are doing, or you can watch for those nonverbal signs of arousal. Some women don't like to talk during foreplay and some get really turned on by it–you will have to judge this by her response to you.

If you are looking for more subtle bodily signs, she may exhibit any of the following or a combination of them: pupils dilating; dry heat emanating from her chest or upper body; flush on the checks, neck, or upper body; chills or goose bumps on any part of her body; harder or accelerated breathing; or small passionate noises or low moans coming from deep in her chest.

You can usually tell when someone is getting turned on by how she is acting. Let the passion build. Don't just take her and throw her down somewhere the minute she shows signs of being aroused, unless she asks you to.

Foreplay, the next step to passion

When your partner starts exhibiting signs of arousal, she may be open to you touching her more intimately. Depending on how she is acting, you might rub her back with the tips of your fingers while lightly kissing her face or neck, or gently massage her arms or legs. Don't just grab her breasts or genitals or force your tongue down her throat. Pay attention to her signals. If they increase, like heavier breathing, more noises, etcetera, then you are still pleasing her.

If you are both inexperienced, she may not know what to do next and she could get scared. Just remain calm, keep doing whatever seems to be working, and remember if she says no, stop right then. Never force anyone to do anything, unless it is part of a sex game that you both have previously agreed upon.

As things heat up, literally, your partner may put your hand where she wants it, or you may have to take the initiative. Depending on if you are standing, sitting, or lying down at this point, ease your hand into her shirt, lightly rubbing her back or stomach, teasing her breasts every now and then. Some women really love their breasts rubbed and some could care less. One of my partners could have an orgasm from that alone. Kiss her lightly as you are massaging near her breasts, then increase your pressure on her mouth, moving down to her neck and shoulders. If she seems receptive to that, then you can either leave her shirt on or take it off, but you need to get where you can put your mouth on her skin.

The move to sexual intimacy

From this point on it is assumed that you are using the safer sex practices listed in Chapter 2. It is up to you to make sure you have the gloves, dental dams, plastic wrap, condoms, or whatever you need to protect both yourself and your partner in the place where you plan to make love with her. You might want to have these ready in a drawer next to the bed, under a pillow, or somewhere handy. It's better to plan ahead than to say in a heated moment, "Gotta go get the safer sex stuff. Be right back!" and then run around the house like a horn-dog in heat, rummaging through kitchen drawers for plastic wrap, and digging through your closet for your latex gloves. Nothing chills me more than to have my partner leave the energy that we have created, so be ready for whatever may come up.

At this time you may want to move to where you've stored your safe-sex kit, like a soft couch, piles of blankets in front of a roaring fireplace, or a fluffy bed. Standing up and making love can be hot, but for the first time it might be a little more intimate to be able to relax. Just make sure if you share your house with other people that no one else is going to come bursting through the door. There's nothing worse than having someone walk in while you are half-naked and down on your girlfriend! Believe me, I know.

After moving to the place you've decided on, kiss your partner and either open her shirt or remove it before you lie down beside her. You can do this slowly, rubbing the tips of your fingers up her back as you remove her shirt, or just about rip the shirt off and fall onto the bed with her. It depends on the situation. If your partner seems shy, or inhibited about her body, it may be better to begin making love to her with her clothes partially on so that she doesn't feel totally exposed. Lie down next to her. If you are right-handed you should be on her right side, and if you are left-handed you should be on her left side. This is pretty important, because you definitely want to be using your dominant hand in this situation.

On to the breasts

Tease her a bit more, lightly skimming the areolae of her breasts with the back of your nails. Watch for goose bumps. She may respond by putting her arms around your back and pulling you to her, or she may just lie there and enjoy what you are doing. You can start kissing her neck and shoulders again, gently nipping her with your teeth, while continuing to massage her. Start moving your mouth down towards her breasts. You can use the tip of your tongue, or you can use your lips to nibble her, but be careful of getting too turned on and biting her. This is not Vampire Time at the OK Corral.

You have to remember that while she is getting turned on, so are you, so keep your passion in check enough to be able to judge her responses. Watch how she reacts to what you are doing. If she starts squirming around and makes you stop, then you may be tickling her, and tickling is probably not what you want to do at this very moment.

Gently circle one of her nipples with your mouth. Sometimes it is nice to do the same thing to the other breast with your fingers. See how she is reacting. Is she still breathing hard? Are her nipples responding with hardness? Are her hands clutching at your back or is she kind of just lying there? If she is exhibiting increased passion, then you can probably begin to actually suck her areola into your mouth, gently flicking the nipple with your tongue. You can practice different techniques to see what she responds to most. Some women like their breasts lightly rubbed with the palms of your hands, while others like them yanked and sucked on like a milking machine. Sometimes they will tell you what they like, and sometimes they won't. Just keep checking to make sure she isn't losing interest.

Moving down south

While you are working on her breasts with your mouth and tongue, you can begin to move your hand down her body. Lightly rub her stomach, around the outside of her hips, and the tops of her thighs. Pay close attention to her breathing. If the rate increases, you can gently rub her inner thigh. If she opens her legs, she is nearly ready for you to be truly with her.

She might at this point grab your hand and place it on her mons pubis. Tease her a bit, don't just jump in it. She will love you for it all the more. If her clothes are still partially on, you can probably move back up and unzip her pants. Tease around her bare skin while doing this. Don't rush it. If she has on underwear, gently play under the elastic at the waist. While you are doing all this stuff, you should be also kissing her mouth or breasts. Remember ambidextrous is great but ambiSEXtrous is better!

If you are kissing her mouth, now is a good time to think about what you are going to do to her when you take off her pants. If you are going to go down on her, you might want to practice a bit on her mouth. Gently suck her lips, then run the tip of your tongue over them, and maybe between them and her gums. This usually turns women on big time, because they know that you are going to do the same thing to them somewhere else. Just do this as a tease. Don't lap her face like a basset hound, or make her think that you are cleaning her mouth with your tongue. And make sure you swallow a lot. Don't be giving her a saliva bath. Basically, don't get too over exuberant, unless she really gets into it.

Like I said before, go with what she is showing you. If she seems to not like something you are doing, move on to something else.

Run your fingers over her pants or underwear, teasing over her mons pubis. If she is really responding, you can either have her help you slip her clothes off, or you can sit back up and take them off yourself. It just depends on the moment, but sometimes it is good to have your lover take your clothes off. If she is too shy to remove her clothes at this time, you may have to resort to slipping your hand down her pants and stimulating her. This is a little difficult, but it can be done. Just don't force her to do what she is not ready for.

If she takes her clothes off and then becomes hesitant or shy, then get under the sheets, or cover her with a blanket. Cuddle up to her, and go with what she is showing you. You might have to take a couple of steps back, doing a bit more kissing on her face, neck, hands, etcetera, or she might let you resume where you were. See what she wants, either by her body's response or by what she is saying.

When her passion is back up again, work on her breasts a bit more, kissing her passionately; then glide your hand over her stomach. Enjoy the electricity of her body. You may be able to feel it coming into your palm. Tease around her thighs a bit while kissing her mouth like you want to kiss her down there.

Gently rub over her mons pubis, feel her soft hair. This is where the magic is—when you first touch her there and feel her love being poured out of her body. If you did everything right, and she is way up on the plateau of arousal, she may be wet when you touch her. Some women get soaked and others just lightly mist. You can feel this with latex gloves on, so don't think you will miss the sensation.

Stay with her, look into her eyes, this is the most amazing feeling of being alive. Tell her whatever you need to say from your heart as you move your fingers slowly into her folds. Rub her gently at first, either up and down, or from side to side. Experiment and see what she likes. Keep gently teasing her with your mouth. Match the slow strokes your hand is making to the slow strokes of your tongue running down her arm and sucking her fingers, or in her mouth or on her breasts. You can make her totally come this way if you aren't quite ready to go down on her.

You should be able to feel her clitoris, although sometimes it will hide. It will feel like a small hard pea within her folds. You can rub it in a circular motion and then slide down into the outside of her opening. This place is extremely sensitive and it usually feels exquisite to be _lightly_ massaged on the outside, just teasing her by letting the tips of one or two of your fingers barely go inside. Continue slowly doing this for a few moments.

She should be quite responsive now, her passion should be way up, and she may be biting your lips, clutching at your back, moaning, talking, or doing a host of other things. Follow her lead. If she opens her legs wide and asks you to go inside with your fingers then do it. Some women like to be penetrated at this time, and some do not, some like it first and some like it after they have a clitoral orgasm. Ask her what she needs you to do for her, if you are not sure.

Working towards orgasm

You can either go down on her now, or see if you can stimulate her with your hand enough to have an orgasm. It depends on where you are in your relationship. If you have given other women orgasms with your fingers, then you know what to do. Start using that technique on her, slow at first, then either increase pressure or stroke her clitoris faster. See how she is responding. She might need you to do it side to side, up and down, or in a circular motion. You can also hold her inner labia and clitoris between both sets of your closed fingers, and gently massage her. You pretty much have to be sitting up between her legs to do this pleasurable little trick. The most important thing about any kind of clitoral stimulation is repetition. If she starts responding by saying "Oh, God, I'm coming," don't change what you are doing. You can do the same thing faster for a more intense orgasm. Just watch for the signs. Some women have a hard time coming from finger stimulation, so ask her what she likes if she is not responding, or have her show you if she is open enough to do so.

If you decide to go down on her, keep rubbing her slowly, teasing her clitoris and softly probing her opening, while you start kissing down her body. Lick her breasts while you are doing this, and keep going down to her stomach. Kiss around her pubic hair. If she is reacting in a positive way, meaning her legs are open and she is not pulling you back up to her face, keep going down.

Gently spread her legs and lower yourself between them. You can kiss her thighs, teasing your face over her pubic hair, which should be covered with dental dam or plastic wrap. Using your fingers on one or both of your hands, spread her outer labia. You can start moving your tongue up through her crevices, gently flicking her clitoris, and then back down again until you reach her entrance. Do this for a little while, keeping the pace slow. Her hips may be moving with your rhythm, her hands may be tangled in your hair, and she should be pretty much in ecstasy.

As her reactions increase, you can either quicken your strokes and see if she comes, or tease her a bit more. She will

49

let you know if she is coming. Either she will start saying she is, or her body will tighten up and then begin to shudder, or she might thrust against your face in time with her contractions. If she doesn't seem to be able to get over that edge, you can use the fingers on both your hands to gently pull both sides of her labia minora up and apart. This will move the skin of the prepuce off the clitoris. Take the tip of your tongue and in a circular motion move it around her clitoris. Do this in a rhythmic way and make sure you keep contact with her clitoris. You can feel it on your tongue. She may come like this or tell you to do it faster. If she doesn't respond you can either <u>carefully</u> suck her clitoris into your mouth, and start rotating your head while swirling the point of your tongue over it, or you can keep lapping her and insert your fingers into her, either hitting her G-spot (Grafenberg) or gently probing her until she comes. If you do the clitoris trick, be careful not to suck too hard. She will either absolutely love this, or she may not like it. It depends on how sensitive her clitoris is.

The next step to total fulfillment

After she has come from her clitoris, you can either wait a few moments and start all over again. or you may want to move up her body and lay on top of her. If you are practicing safer sex, make sure to either discard the barrier or have it marked so that you can tell which side is which, in case you need to use it again. If you are not practicing safer sex and you move up on top of her, you may also want to have a damp washcloth near so that you can wipe your mouth and chin. Some women, especially straight ones, can get totally grossed out if you kiss them right after being down on them. Others might not mind at all, but a washcloth is a handy thing to have. While you are moving up, you could slide your fingers inside. Her body should be totally ready for this as long as her mind goes along.

Some women don't like this and others absolutely love it. If your lover feels a bit overwhelmed by the feeling, you might try lying beside her and entering her that way. To me, there is no feeling in the world as amazing as being inside the woman you love, so hopefully she will be receptive to it.

You can move your hand in and out or in a slow rotation. You can also turn your hand so that the palm is towards whatever she is lying on and gently thrust downward. A lot of women like this because it stimulates the rectum without having to go directly inside of it. As her passion responds to what you are doing, you should start increasing your rhythm. She should be moving with you at this point. As you come to a crescendo, you can curve your fingers up, towards her stomach if she is on her back, and hit her G-spot. The texture will usually feel different than the vaginal wall, and she will go absolutely wild when you hit it. You can either keep thrusting with your fingers curved up, or you can stop thrusting and just move your curved fingers faster, hitting her spot until she has an amazing orgasm. She may or may not ejaculate at this point. If she does, it is totally normal, so don't freak out. It will smell a little stronger than her regular scent and the consistency will be like water, but it is not usually urine.

Most women are unaware that they have this capability, so your partner may be embarrassed if this happens, but assure her that this is normal. If a woman is so turned on that she ejaculates, it is the biggest compliment you could ever get as a lover. It puts you in the realm of electrical equipment, like vibrators, so be proud of yourself and your lover. Just get a towel and use safer sex.

For you guys reading this, by the time you get to this level of arousal, and your lover has had several orgasms, she might be open to you penetrating her and having one of your own. The complaint I have heard from straight women over and over again is that after their man has his orgasm he turns over and goes to sleep or he leaps out of the bed to get some water or take a leak. This is not good, especially if you haven't taken care of your partner's needs first. She's just lying there, dissatisfied at first, which can eventually turn into anger and a possible breakup, or a complete shutdown of her affections toward you.

From what I've been told, most penises are not curved to reach a woman's G-spot, and there is very little stimulation to the clitoris from just mounting her and carrying on like a wild hunching dog. So wisen up and talk to your partner and find out what she needs. If you just do the ol' hump and pump, you are also missing out on something that is totally awesome and fulfilling. While in the midst of your own orgasm, it is doubtful that you will be able to feel her body respond to your every touch, and this is what the difference of truly making love and just having sex is. It is so incredible to be fully aware when you are making love with a woman, and to actually utilize all of your parts instead of just one, especially if that one part just doesn't fit her perfectly.

Most women are very capable of having multiple orgasms, so making love can go on for hours, or until one of you gets too tired to move. On the other hand, if you or your lover has problems achieving orgasm, make sure to read the rest of this chapter. There is more than one way to skin the kitty, as they say.

Some other techniques and positions

In lovemaking just about anything you can think of can be done, if both partners are willing and able. Using lots of positions and making love in different places are two ways to keep your relationship young at heart. Since I am not the Kama Sutra Goddess, I will just list a few of the more basic ones here. The rest is up to you. Be as wild and brave as possible and you will become a great lover.

Side-to-side

This position is good, especially if you need to be stealthy for some reason—like your lover's sister is sound asleep in the same room, also known as being young and kind of dumb, or some other unusual circumstance.

The two facing partners lie on their sides, stimulating each other with their hands or penetration with sex toys or penis. If just using your hands, this can be done by taking turns or in unison. If you need to be really quiet, then it should probably be one at a time. Use good sense and don't get caught in a compromising position.

Standing up

This arrangement can be very wild so it's good to be against a wall for stability. You can either be face-to-face with your partner while your hands are doing the work, or you can be down on your knees with your mouth and fingers having a little "crotchety" party. If you are doing the latter, be warned. Safer sex is pretty hard in this position, unless your partner has on adult-sized plastic training pants.

Straddling

This position is when one partner is lying on her back, and the other is straddling her lap or stomach. The person lying down can be stimulating her partner either clitorally or vaginally. The partner on top can also move her body against her lover, known as tribadism or grinding, which will stimulate her clitoris, or move her body with her lover's fingers or a dildo/penis inside of her.

Sitting up

This is a highly erotic position that can be done in a roomy chair, on a couch, on the floor, or in the bed. It is kind of nice if you've just given your partner an oral orgasm, to sit up and pull her into your lap. You can put one arm around her back for support, have your fingers, or a sex toy or penis, deep inside of her, curved towards her stomach and hitting her G-spot, and be kissing her passionately all at the same time. She can also choose to move her body on you, hitting all the right spots and giving your tired arm muscles a rest.

Sitting up—on your partner's face

Speaking of erotic, if your knees and thighs can handle this position, you can come like a wild coconut-humpin' monkey! You can do this straddling your partner's head frontwards or backwards. She can put her fingers in you, and at the same time you can move your body on her mouth for the ultimate clitoral orgasm. A little warning though. Safe sex in this position is difficult, but it can be done. Just be careful not to smother your partner with the latex or plastic barrier. Another thing is to make sure your partner knows what you mean when you ask her to sit on your face. I heard one story of a poor woman who was almost suffocated when her inexperienced lover plopped down on her face like she was sitting on a fluffy love seat.

The ol' 69

Lots of people joke around about doing 69, but few lesbians can really do it right. If you don't know what it is, just look at the number—it's both partners performing oral action at the same time. Now you can do this on your sides, or one on top of the other, but it is not the easiest position in the world. I think it's harder for most of us because our vaginas are a little difficult to get to. Unless you happen to be with Janice the Giraffe-Necked Woman, I would say leave 69 to the people who are best at it, or use it for some fun foreplay.

From behind

This position can be done either with one partner on her knees and the other one behind her, or one partner lying on her side or stomach with the other stimulating her from behind. Depending on the circumstances, this position can either be totally erotic, or totally threatening. I was pretty much raped by a woman this way one time, and it freaked me out because I had no way to get out from under her weight. She did not pay attention to the fact that I was really having a problem, and I never trusted her intimately again.

If you want to try making love from behind, make sure to discuss it, or if it is something that naturally happens one time when you are together, just make sure that your partner is OK with this kind of vulnerability.

Anal sex

Some people love anal sex and others can't stand it. I have one bisexual woman friend who would rather have anal sex than vaginal intercourse. It just depends on the person. This is another communication issue. Just don't go cramming something in your partner's rectum unless you know for sure this is what she wants.

If you decide you'd like to try anal sex, it's best to start out small, say with one well-lubricated finger. Finger cots are great for anal sex and some sort of protection should always be used. As with vaginal sex, start out slowly and see how your lover responds. She might like you to swirl your finger in a circular motion on the outside and then slowly move in, or she might like a bit of pumping action. If you are entering her from behind, you can have one finger in her anus and the thumb of your other hand in her vagina with your index finger stimulating her clitoris. Talk about being filled up! Just remember, never use toys or fingers in the anus and then in the vagina. This is a sure-fire way of giving your partner the biggest, nastiest infection of her life, so always use fresh condoms or wash your toys with soap and hot water between activities. Make sure if they are battery operated toys that you do not get water inside the battery compartment. The contacts will rust and you will have a vibrator that doesn't vibrate. Also, do not insert small objects into the anus, because they have a way of disappearing. You sure don't want to spend the night in the emergency room explaining how your partner's ring got lodged way up inside your butt.

The illusive and unusual scissors

Well, I can't say much about this position, especially since I've never successfully done it. The two partners are supposed to be able to straddle each other and mutually rub their vulvas together, stimulating each other to a wonderful mutual clitoral orgasm. Kind of like two Vs meeting in the middle at their crotches. All I can say is good luck and more power to you if you can get off doing this. I ended up with a bruise the size of a half dollar from my partner's pubic bone slamming into mine, and this is not anything I'd want to do again. I do know some women who love this position, but if you decide to try it, do so with caution.

Butt to butt

This unusual position works best when using a double-headed dildo. Both partners are on their knees, butt to butt, with the dildo inside both of them. If done gently, this can be pretty erotic, but be warned. If one partner gets a little too energetic, her movement can cause the other side of the dildo to go too deep into her partner, causing pain and possible injury. I knew of two women who were using a double-header and got a little too energetic. The dildo slipped and one of the women ended up having her perineum torn apart. She had to go to the emergency room and have it stitched up, a rather embarrassing and painful situation. Use all vibrators and toys cautiously as described in the next section.

Adult toys—let's take the pleasure a step further

Some women like toys and others are too proud to admit that they might. I feel that anything which enhances your time together, or alone, is

Various dildos and battery-operated toys

perfectly OK. Besides, it can be really nice after a hard-core love-making session to get out the ol' vibrator and watch your lover have five more orgasms before she falls deeply asleep in your arms.

Sometimes, women find it hard to have an orgasm from hand or mouth stimulation and need a vibrator. If this is true for you or your partner, don't be embarrassed about it. Just be honest so that no one feels they are not a good enough lover to make the other person come. Have regular foreplay, then let the vibrator become an extension of yourself.

What's the best kind of vibrator?

Depending on where and what you want to stimulate, there are many types and styles of vibrators to choose from. There are some that use electricity and others that use batteries; some look like penises, bananas, and even cats, and some are smooth and look like little rockets. There are some that are curved to hit the G-spot, and there are

The Jett

some like little butterflies that you can wear inside your clothes.

You can buy vibrators and dildos at some home lingerie parties, or your local adult store. Silicone is always the best material for any kind of adult toy. Because it is nonporous, it doesn't harbor bacteria and can be easily cleaned with antibacterial soap and hot water. If you can't imagine walking into a sex store, you can buy adult toys online or by mail order (see the index for a list of suppliers).

The best toy I've found for multiple clitoral orgasms is the regular handheld massager that you can buy at almost any drug store. I have one I call "The Jett," and I swear it could about make a dead person come. These handheld massagers usually have several attachments, which you can experiment with. The bell-shaped one, shown in the illustration, seems to work the best for me. You can either place it on the top or either side of your prepuce, because it is too strong to put directly on the clitoris.

The most important thing when using one of these vibrators is that you should be as dry as possible in your outer vulva area. If the revolutions per minute are fast enough, it can burn you, so use a dry towel and wipe yourself off before placing the vibrator near your delicate parts. If it is too strong use some soft cloth between you and the vibrator. Also, these things can be powerful enough to cause a woman to ejaculate. Make sure not to do this on the vibrator! Remember, this is an electrical appliance. It can short-out or shock you if you soak it down, so don't be using it in the tub either. I sure don't want to read about your untimely, orgasmic death on the front page of some rag magazine at the local supermarket. So use good sense and put a towel between you and the vibrator if you think you might rain all over the place. If you are using the vibrator on your partner, also have plastic wrap along with the towel, to keep it safe for both of you.

Another thing you can do with a handheld massager is use it with a hollow dildo. Find the attachment that best fits inside of the dildo and turn it on while it's inside of you or your partner. This can produce a very intense orgasm, especially if you have it angled up towards the G-spot, or down towards the rectum, which also stimulates the clitoris. If you use a handheld vibrator in this way, lubrication is a must, along with a condom for switching out if with a partner. The dildo will take most of the rpm, so it should not burn anyone who is using it. Just make sure to protect the vibrator from getting wet. You can also use a dildo or internal vibrator while performing oral sex for a double orgasm—whatever you and your partner are in the mood for.

Does wanting to use a dildo mean I might be a closet straight?

No, it doesn't. What it does mean is that you might need more to fill you than a few fingers. Remember, we are women living in physical bodies that have their own needs. Just because you would like something bigger inside of you does not mean anything about being straight. It just means you like to feel filled up.

Now some women like this all the time, and some never want anything, like fingers or dildos, inside of them. That's perfectly OK too. You have to decide if it is something you can live without doing. If you have the constant urge to be inside the woman you love, or to perform any other kind of sexual activity, and she will not allow you to do what you yearn to do, it can have dire consequences on your relationship.

To be a great lover, you have to be able to go with what your partner needs. If she begs you to strap one on and do her from behind, then it is up to you to decide if you can or not. This comes back to communication. Discuss new things you want to do before you are at that point in the heat of passion. Nothing can be more disappointing than fantasizing all day about some radical new position or toy, only to have your lover say, "No way!"

If you find that you or your partner is having chronic sexual difficulties, you might want to read the section at the end of this chapter concerning the signs of and how to handle childhood sexual abuse issues.

Shower heads

Another fun way to have clitoral orgasms, either by yourself or with a partner, is with a pulsating shower massage. Make sure the water is not too hot, and always have the stream of water pointing down across your clitoris and away from your vaginal opening. Some of these shower massagers are very powerful, so NEVER point the stream up into your vagina. You could get a nasty infection or even worse an injury, so use caution when using water appliances.

Other ways of being sexual

Trisexuals, the three-way affair

Threesomes, hmmm, what can I say? Have I ever done it? Yes. Would I do it again? No. Why? It was just too weird the next morning, and when it got out to the small Southern lesbian community I was a part of at that time, my lover and I were completely shunned.

Now I'm sure times have changed since the early eighties, but I'm not sure how much. I will say this, if you are in the beginning of a relationship, I would not suggest having a threesome. It just puts too much stress on a growing partnership. If you are out being wild and sowing your oats, using safer sex all the time, then maybe you can handle it. It just depends on who you are and what you want.

As with most other forms of human sexuality, I have nothing against threesomes. The upside was it was erotic, and it was fun. The downside was it tore my relationship of seven years apart and ruined a nice friendship I had with the woman who was our third party.

It also surprised me how other lesbians reacted when they found out. I was picked up and groped by a butch weight-lifter at a Metropolitan Community Church volleyball game, publicly humiliated at an art show where I was exhibiting, and totally ostracized from a community who expects everyone else not to ostracize them. It was a hard lesson I learned in my early twenties and one I don't wish to repeat. If you decide to have a threesome, just be forewarned. At least in my case, the pain totally outweighed the pleasure.

Fetishes

A fetish is usually something that causes sexual arousal. It may be anything from wearing spike-heeled boots or leather or rubber clothing, to looking at certain body parts or even cucumbers sold at your local market. Sometimes fetishists require that their object be present during sex to achieve an orgasm, or they may have to fantasize about it in order to heighten their arousal to bring on an orgasm. Having a fetish is not bad, unless it is something that freaks out your partner. Again, communication is the issue here. If you have a fetish that is too bizarre for words, you may want to just visualize it instead of making it a part of your sex play with someone else.

Sadism and masochism (S&M)

Sadism is defined as an intentional infliction of pain or humiliation which brings on arousal and sexual excitement. Masochism means getting sexually aroused from being hurt or humiliated. I guess you can see what a perfect fit these two types of people are and why their relationship is called S&M.

The word sadism comes from the French author, Marquis DeSade, who wrote about using cruelty for sexual gratification in the late 1700s. The word "masochism" was named after Leopold Baron Von Sacher-Masoch. He wrote *Venus in Furs* in 1888, which was all about the pleasures of pain.

I have known some people who are into mild forms of S&M, that included spankings, master-slave relationships, and some forms of bondage. As with everything else in this book, I believe that whatever two consenting adults do in private is certainly none of my business. If you love being turned over your partner's knee and smacked on your bare butt, more power to you.

On the other hand, I have known people who took S&M to extremes and actually brutalized their lovers until they could no longer function as regular human beings. They became like chained dogs, totally dependent on their "master" or "mistress." I'm not so sure how good it is to be tied up in a tub of freezing water and have a live 8-foot boa constrictor thrown on you, or spend hours chained to a bed with a spiked dog collar choking you if you move.

I do believe some of the more intense forms of cruelty stem directly from the reenactment of childhood abuse. Whether this is on a conscious or subconscious level, it really doesn't matter. What does matter is the fact that a relationship like this usually ends in someone getting hurt or even killed. If the abused person escapes, it can end in years of therapy or finding another person who will fill her needs to be punished.

Just like everything in life, a little can be great, but a lot can be detrimental to your mental or physical health. If you find that you are having fantasies of physically maiming someone for sexual pleasure, it might stem from something that happened to you when you were a child. The same goes for if you have constant fantasies of being terribly hurt to achieve an orgasm. In either case, you might want to read the next section or seek professional help.

Childhood abuse: sexual, physical, and emotional

It is a known fact that at least one in four females and one in six males are subjected to some kind of childhood sexual abuse. Since I am a member of the one in four females group, I take ending child abuse personally. Abuse was a large part of my daily life growing up, and it took me years to recover as an adult. I still have problems to this day, and believe me I've been through lots of therapy and read many self-help books.

I believe child abuse is the number one reason we have so much crime in today's world. It is a horrible heritage that has been passed down for generations, and it is up to us to stop it.

Now some people will balk at what I'm about to write, but I totally believe my soul chose to be born into child abuse so that I could do something about it when I grew up. All of my novels have characters who are survivors and have flourished as adults, just like I have. These books are written for the one out of four of us who need a positive role model, someone who made it through the hell of her past

I know this is a hard subject to think about; it's hard for

me to admit that it happened to me, but if we don't think about it and learn what the signs are, then nothing will change. Look around you. One in four of your female friends has experienced some sort of abuse. That's just too much! We don't talk about it. We sweep it under some moldy rug somewhere, where it grows into something that can no longer be hidden. When the flashbacks and fear of abandonment start, they can ruin your relationship with the person you love most. Listen to what I am saying here, because my first two serious relationships ended because I was too emotionally sick to know I needed help.

What is considered sexual abuse?

Sexual abuse takes many forms. These are some of the more common: inappropriate touching or kissing of your genitals; being fondled, kissed, or held on the lap of someone with an erection; raped rectally or vaginally; shown sexual magazines or movies; any kind of ritualized S&M whether sexual or not; being ridiculed concerning the development of your body; being talked to in a sexually inappropriate way; or being forced to be a child prostitute or pose for pornographic movies or photos.

Sometimes people remember what happened and sometimes they don't. If you or your lover is exhibiting some of the following symptoms, there may be a reason to investigate your past a little deeper, with either a qualified therapist or counselor.

Symptoms of childhood sexual abuse

There are many symptoms of sexual abuse including the following: the need to control everything about sex; problems being close in nonsexual ways; confusing sex with affection; being the absolute best in everything sexual (that's why I could write this chapter); experiencing flashbacks of abuse when making love; getting aroused by thinking about sexual abuse; having a hard time trusting anyone; not staying emotionally with your partner when making love, meaning you are thinking of anything else but what is going on; having fear of having children or being overprotective of children; experiencing recurring thoughts that you don't deserve to be with anyone; suffering from abandonment issues—always fearing someone will leave you; feeling you are different from others; having intense fear or terror when you think about being intimate; hating yourself or feeling the need to kill yourself; being scared of success or failure; experiencing frequent nightmares; being fearful of violence or of being violent or abusive to someone else; having any kind of eating disorder; avoiding sex altogether; thinking that sex is disgusting or dirty; having the inability to set limits, whether sexual or not; feeling taken advantage of in all of your relationships; or dating someone who is like your abuser either physically or emotionally.

These are just some of the symptoms of childhood sexual abuse. During my life I have had thirteen of these symptoms, although I only have a couple of them occasionally now. One thing I do know is if I can heal, so can you.

If you had any kind of abuse when you were little, it affected you whether you realize it or not. I did not know how much it hurt me until I was in my twenties. I would be with my partner, and just about to have an orgasm, when I would have a total flashback of my uncle going down on me at four years old. Talk about an orgasm leaving in a hurry. That's what it felt like. One second it was there, the next it dissolved into the past, leaving me with chronic fear that was coiled in my stomach—which eventually turned into an ulcer.

This is the type of thing that sneaks up on you when you least expect it. This is the gift of child abuse, but you can choose to do something about it. You will always have those memories but they don't have to ruin your whole life. Choose to be healthy. Choose to break the pattern of mental illness. Choose your life. Success is the best revenge against something so horrible. Use your gifts. Turn your pain around and do something for yourself and the world.

If you don't feel like you can discuss what happened to you with a therapist, then go get *The Courage to Heal* book and workbook by Ellen Bass and Laura Davis. It helped me more than all of my years of therapy combined. It made me realize how much the abuse affected the life I am living now, and it helped me to change the patterns that resulted in all of my failed intimate relationships. The book was coauthored by a lesbian, so it is totally friendly for anyone who wants to take back the control in her life from her abuser.

If you are the type of person who needs to understand why child abuse happens, the best book I ever read on the subject was *Bradshaw on the Family* by John Bradshaw. This book discusses how family patterns are passed down from one generation to the next. It made it very clear for me to see how my childhood was destroying my adult life, and it gave me ways to stop the patterns that were ingrained in me.

If you were physically, mentally, or sexually abused as a child, these patterns can sneak up on you and surface as abuse in your adult relationships. Since this is more common than most of us would like to admit, I've included the following section to illustrate the forms of abuse some of us may be living in.

Domestic Partner Abuse

Abuse in an adult relationship can be defined as any behavior your partner uses to control you, which causes physical, sexual and/or psychological damage, or causes you to live in fear. The following are some types of partner abuse:

Emotional Abuse

This is a painful kind of abuse where your partner puts you down, calls you names, and generally makes you feel bad about yourself to your face or in front of other people. She may play mind games to make you think it is your problem or tell you that you are crazy or stupid. She may encourage self-hatred about being who you are or force you to be closeted. She may use blackmail to control you, treat you like a servant, or threaten murder or suicide so that you are too afraid for your own life, or hers, to make a change.

Isolation

When an abuser uses isolation, he is controlling what you do, such as who you see and talk to, or where you go. He may not allow you to be involved in your community, and he may sabotage any new friendships that you try to form outside of the relationship. The abusive partner may use jealousy to justify his actions.

Intimidation and Threats

This kind of abuse usually begins at home, but as your abuser gains confidence of her control of you she may do some of the following in public situations: using looks, actions, or gestures to make you afraid; driving unsafely when you are in the car to scare you; destroying your general possessions or cherished items; abusing pets or children; buying weapons and showing them to you; or threatening to "out you" at work or to your friends or family.

Physical Abuse

This abuse usually happens in the privacy of your home and can include pushing, biting, hitting, punching, using a weapon, or forcing you to participate in sex. If you try to flee, your abuser may attempt to confine you physically. If you are injured, your abuser may prevent you from going to a doctor, or he may control your food or medication. If you are severely injured, your abuser may take you to a hospital, but threaten you with further physical abuse if you do not lie about what happened. He may say he is directly related to you, and accompany you to the examining room. He may speak for you and not allow you to be alone with a health-care practitioner.

Sexual Abuse

Sexual abuse can take many forms, but generally it is defined as any sexual activity that is unwanted or coerced. Also included are non-disclosure of STD/HIV status; sexual name calling; accusations of you wanting to have or having sex with other people; or your abuser may threaten to have sex with others or force you to become pregnant or to terminate an existing pregnancy.

Using Children

If you have children, your abuser may use them to keep you in control. Some ways of doing this are: threatening to expose your relationship so that your children are taken away; telling your children bad things about you; using visitation of the other parent to harass you; making sarcastic remarks about your parenting abilities; or refusing to allow you to see your children if you don't have full custody.

Economic Abuse

When an abuser controls you economically he may prevent you from getting or keeping a job outside the home, and demand that you ask for money or an allowance from him. If you are allowed to work, he may take any money you make. He may not allow you to participate in financial decision-making, or may deny your rights to any assets within the partnership. He may threaten to act out at your work place so that you lose your job and are financially dependent upon him.

Patterns of abuse and abuser justification

Abuse and abusers follow a pattern of gradual escalation. The abuse usually starts out slowly with harsh criticisms, then apologies. At first the incidents happen without any regular frequency. Then they escalate. It doesn't matter which form of abuse is employed. Eventually it escalates until the abuse is the norm and those periods of getting along are few and far between. Most people react by objecting to abuse, and their partner may verbally and/or physically respond.

When an abuser reaches a point that he knows you have been pushed too far, or that he has frightened himself by the violence he has perpetrated, his reaction may be to say that he didn't mean to be abusive. He may make light of the abuse and blame you for his behavior. When asked about the abuse, he may say that it didn't happen, or that you are the one who is abusive. He may blame stress as a problem or say he had a traumatic childhood. He may use drinking or drug abuse as an excuse, or say that society oppresses him. He may say he can't control his anger, or that he can't express his feelings appropriately.

Since abuse is usually something that builds slowly, the abused begins to make excuses for the abuser and take blame herself. She may also be seduced by how romantic or attentive her partner becomes and want with all her heart to believe that this is the reality of the relationship, that this is how her partner really is. The reality is that the longer the process is allowed to continue, the norm becomes abuse and the exceptions are the good times.

No matter what the excuse is, abuse is wrong. All of us experience life's problems, but we don't go around beating or belittling everyone else in order to cope. Abusive people are using control to get their own way and to keep their partners under their thumbs. They CAN control their abuse, but choose to control another person instead.

How you may feel:

If you are in an abusive relationship, you may be ashamed to tell anyone. This is especially bad if you are lesbian and your friends or family do not know, which can lead to feelings of depression, humiliation, and increased isolation. Many abused women blame themselves, thinking that they have failed the relationship in some way, such as not being a good enough lover, partner, or parent. They may feel guilty or scared to leave their partner. Many hold on to the hope that their partner will change. This is often reinforced with apologies after the abuse has taken place like "I swear it will never happen again," or "I promise it won't—please don't leave me." When the abuse happens again, it sets up a pattern where the abuser knows she has gotten away with it one time, so she thinks she can do it over and over again.

So why do women remain in abusive relationships? Some believe they can't leave because they are not financially secure. Others think that the abuse wouldn't be happening if they didn't deserve it. In most cases, this last belief comes directly from childhood abuse.

When we were growing up, many of us were taught that adults are always right. "I brought you into this world, and I can take you out" was a very common statement in my childhood home. To many kids this translates to "If Mom and Dad are beating me and threatening my life, then something must be wrong with me," or "I must have done something wrong." This can set up a pattern in your adult years where you view, or you subconsciously view, anyone who abuses you as acting in a correct way. It can lead you to believe that you are responsible for your partner's violence, but this is simply not true.

No matter what happened when you were little, abuse in any form is WRONG. It is up to you to change the way you think of it. Now whether this means finding a good therapist and working on it, or getting the *The Courage to Heal Workbook, For Women and Men Survivors of Child Sexual Abuse*, it is up to you to do something to make a change.

Things you can do:

The most important thing you can do is pay attention to how you feel. If you are in a new relationship and you find a pattern of abuse developing, talk to staff at a spouse abuse shelter, a counselor, or a friend. You can also do research at the library or on the Internet to verify your feelings. Check the index for some some websites where you can find support and help.

If you want to work on the relationship, you and your partner both need to get into some kind of therapy or couples counseling. If you feel safe, you can discuss this with her. Abuse is a behavior that can be hard to change, but abusers can change if they realize how detrimental it is not only to their partner but to themselves as well.

There should always be a safe place for you to go if the abuser reverts to his old ways. You may have to rely on friends or family. Have your friends or family be present if you need to see your abuser for any reason. Have a code word that you can use to notify them if he suddenly shows up, or that things are not so good and you need help. Change your phone number and door locks and have an answering machine to screen all of your calls.

If your relationship has developed into an abusive one and

you want to get out of it permanently, you may no longer have any friends or family contacts. It may also be that if you do have friends or family still in your life, your abuser may have threatened their safety to control you.

If things get really bad—physical assault, sexual assault, threats, or stalking—you may have to talk to the police about legal options such as a restraining order or criminal charges. Some states charge for a restraining order, but some will waive the cost if you can't afford to pay.

Make a detailed plan to escape. Leave when your abuser is not at home and take clothing and personal items you may need. If you have family or friends and they haven't been threatened, you may be able to use them for a safe house. If you don't feel it is safe to go to your family or friends, call a local spouse abuse shelter and ask for help and a place to stay. Most shelters have safe houses. Some admit people who have only experienced physical abuse and some will take you in if you have experienced verbal abuse. Once at the shelter you will be safe, and the staff there can help with counseling, community resources, legal advice, and assistance in filing a restraining order.

Your life is up to you. Either be a victim and let your abuser win, or use your gifts and be the success you are meant to be. You have to be strong enough to release the past, and brave enough to change the pattern that was ingrained in you from your youth. Only we can stop the abuse and become the incredible people we are meant to be. I'm sitting at my keyboard typing the truth of my life, in hopes that maybe what happened to me can help you, or someone you know, to make a move towards healing. Take back your power now, and turn it into something beautiful.

If you think your relationship could use some counseling, the next chapter will help you and your partner know what to expect.

CHAPTER 5

Counseling from a therapist's point of view

Introduction

Since many people are unfamiliar with counseling, I have prepared this chapter to help you know what to expect if you choose to work with a counselor or therapist. Included is information for counselors who may be working with lesbians and gay men.

—K.W.

Your options for counseling

You may go to a private therapist or a community mental health center. There are many pros and cons to both depending upon your needs. If you work during the day, evening appointments fit better with your schedule. Some private therapists offer this service, but most agencies do not. If you are interested in or have been recommended to use group therapy, community mental health centers have this option, while private therapists may or may not run groups.

Finding and setting up an appointment with a private therapist

If you choose to see a private therapist, I suggest that you ask people you know if they could recommend someone. If you don't feel comfortable asking friends, private therapists are sometimes listed in your local weekly or lesbian/gay papers.

When you decide on a therapist, you need to contact their office to see if they are accepting new clients, or if there is a long waiting period before you can set up an appointment. If they are accepting new clients, you can ask to interview your prospective new therapist to see if you feel comfortable. A counseling relationship is like any other relationship—you're either going to click with the person or you're not. It's better to get a feel for a therapist before you decide to schedule an appointment with her, and you can do this by phone.

During the interview, you can ask questions about her style of counseling such as: does she follow a specific counseling theory, and how does this theory work? What would a typical session be like? Tell her your reason to begin therapy, and ask if she is comfortable with the issues you will be discussing. Find out how she will work with you. I would suggest interviewing several private therapists. If you have insurance that covers therapy, ask if she is a provider with your insurance company.

Check with your insurance company, or human resources office, to verify exactly what your counseling benefits cover. Some insurance companies send people to EAP (employee assistance programs). These programs are usually limited to three to six sessions. With EAP programs you are often assigned to a therapist. If the first interview with an EAP therapist determines an issue will take more than three to six sessions, you will most likely be referred to a private therapist who is authorized for reimbursement by your insurance company. If you are referred out, they will either contact the therapist for you or give you the names and numbers so that you can arrange your own appointment. Ask for two to three names so you can interview the EAP providers. Once you settle on a therapist, schedule an appointment for your first session. Depending on your symptoms or issues, the therapist may suggest you consider medication and refer you to a psychiatrist. Some private therapists work alone, while others may be in a group practice that includes a psychiatrist.

Community mental health centers

If you choose to go to a community mental health center, call for an initial appointment. The support staff may or may not ask you the reason you need to see a therapist. If they ask be honest. Your answer may determine with whom your initial counseling appointment will be. If they set up an appointment with a therapist when you call, you should advise them of any preferences you may have concerning your therapist, such as male or female. If they are able, the support staff will try to accommodate your request.

You may be asked to come in and fill out demographic paperwork before you are scheduled to see your new therapist. You will need to disclose basic information about yourself, such as your home address and phone number; information on your employment and health insurance company (if you have health insurance, they will need your card); social security number; basic health information; and why you are seeking counseling. After filling out your paperwork, you may see a therapist for an intake session or you may have to schedule an intake appointment.

The intake will involve you and the therapist evaluating what services the mental health center has that you would benefit from, and if you should consider medication if your symptoms indicate to the therapist that there may be a need. An appointment will then be scheduled for you to meet with a psychiatrist who will be able to write your prescription.

Fees

If you receive services at a community mental health center, the agency has hired your therapist to provide counseling services to you. These services are usually billed per hour. They can be billed as a full fee or on a sliding scale based on your household income. If you have health insurance, it may or may not pay for all or a portion of your appointments.

Check your policy before you go to the mental health facility The support staff should meet with you to determine the cost of the services you will receive and if they accept payment from your insurance company.

There are usually separate charges for individual therapy, group therapy, and appointments with a psychiatrist. The person meeting with you should provide a breakdown of each of these categories. If the cost set for you is beyond your means to pay, let the center know immediately. Sometimes there are procedures in place wherein the center may appeal for a reduction in the cost of the services you will receive, or they may offer to work out a payment plan.

A private therapist may also work on a sliding scale or be willing to work out a payment plan if you do not have insurance coverage, or if the private therapist is not covered by your EAP or insurance company. If you find a therapist you like who is not covered by your insurance, ask about payment options.

Your intake session with a private or community mental health therapist

The first meeting with a therapist will be to review what brings you in, your history, family history, sexual abuse history (if any), and any problems you may have, or have had, with self-harm (suicidality) or harm toward others (homicidality). There may be more questions depending on the therapist, the agency, or the state you reside in. Different states will require agencies to gather some information that others may not. The gathering of your personal information is called an intake.

The therapist will most likely review with you how the issue you are wanting to deal with is affecting your life, and the two of you will set up the goal(s) of your sessions. Goals are sometimes revised as your sessions continue. Remember, in any counseling session, if you don't understand something your therapist says or why she says it, you have the right to ask about it. You also have the right to open a discussion if you don't agree with something the therapist says.

Many therapists will give homework assignments. These are designed to help you continue the work you are doing during your sessions or to expand upon it. These assignments could be to read a specific book (bibliotherapy); to journal, which means keeping track of your thoughts and feelings each day, or what you think and feel about specific issues your therapist assigns to you to write about; or to practice a certain behavior(s). There may also be deep breathing exercises and other assignments that are too numerous to describe. The assignments listed above are some of the more common ones.

The counseling process

I see therapy as a cooperative effort between the therapist and the client. Progress depends on many things including motivation, effort, and other life circumstances such as your interactions with family, friends, and associates. The goals, methods, and treatment should be agreed upon by all involved. These factors may determine the pace of your progress as well as your results. In all settings it is required that clients are given a diagnosis which will become a part of their confidential record. This is because of a combination of state requirements and insurance company requirements.

Your first session

When you have your first session, the therapist will probably discuss your situation and work with you to determine general goals. Like any new relationship, there may be a bit of apprehension or you may feel nervous during your first session. Let the therapist know you are nervous so that she can work with you. After the first few sessions, if you feel there is a personality conflict discuss this with your therapist. See if you can work out any differences. If you and the therapist feel good about the results, you can continue with counseling. If you aren't comfortable, then you can consider finding another therapist. Remember, you are the one who decided to seek help, and you always have the choice to change your mind about who you want to accompany you on your journey.

If you want a family member(s) or significant other to join you in a session, discuss this with your therapist in advance. She will know what you wish to work on in the session, and will probably discuss if this would be constructive for your progress at that point in your treatment.

Some methods used in therapy

There are numerous ways to help someone who is having difficulties such as: relaxation techniques, conflict management, learning effective communication skills, behavioral contracts, and positive self-talk. Your therapist will be happy to answer any questions you may have about therapeutic approaches. Depending on your issues, you may be encouraged to join a group (either treatment or support/self-help such as AA, NA, etc.) or have one-on-one sessions.

Group sessions usually involve five or more people who are experiencing similar situations. One or two therapists may facilitate the sessions, which can deal with depression, emotion regulation, management of symptoms, or coping skills, to name a few. In many cases, group therapy can be a very positive experience. Hearing other people's experiences can help you to understand you're not alone, get support from others who have experienced similar things, and get feedback from others who are supportive and caring concerning your situation.

One-on-one sessions are approximately fifty minutes and involve just you and your therapist. Sometimes the therapist may take notes to focus on key issues. This is so she can review your progress. Session frequency is worked out between you and your therapist.

If you are in an emergency situation, call your therapist. Let her know this is a crisis and how to reach you. After you leave the message and where to call, stay off the phone and stay at home. You'd be surprised how many people will leave a message, then leave home, or get on the phone. Also, keep in mind that your therapist is seeing clients and is usually only free for about ten minutes between each appointment. She will get back to you as soon as she can. If a client does not show up for an appointment, your therapist can possibly spend more than ten minutes with you on the phone.

Sometimes matters get worse before they get better. For example, during the counseling process you may experience feelings such as intense sadness, frustration, anxiety, or guilt. You may find that some relationships become more difficult due to the changes you're making. These experiences are not uncommon and can be surpassed with continued work with your therapist.

Confidentiality

All the information you share with your therapist, and all of your records are confidential. That means that your therapist will not communicate information concerning you and your treatment to any other individual. Your diagnosis, treatment status, or history will not be revealed without a Release of Information form signed by you. Only under special circumstances can a therapist not guarantee confidentiality:

1. If you (and/or your family member or partner) communicate a threat to harm another person

2. If you (and/or your family member or partner) threaten to harm yourself or are unable to care for yourself

3. If your therapist suspects abuse or neglect of a child, helpless adult or an elder, then federal laws mandate your therapist break confidentiality.

Considerations

If you have to cancel an appointment, make sure to call at least twenty-four hours in advance if possible. This will help your therapist schedule someone else for your session who may need it. Also, some agencies will charge you if you do not abide by their cancellation policies, so make sure to ask about the correct procedure during your first visit

If your purpose for seeing a therapist is couples counseling or family counseling, this should be the focus in your sessions. You and your partner, or family members, should not be seeing the same therapist for individual therapy. If a therapist sees you and your partner, or family members, individually this can cause a conflict of interest and possibly lead to your confidentiality being broken. This is not to say that you can't see a therapist for individual issues and occasionally ask for your partner, or your family, to join your sessions to work on specific issues.

Handling complaints

Anytime you find yourself dissatisfied with the counseling process, do not be afraid or intimidated to let your counselor know immediately. She will be willing to work out any difficulties that may arise. If you are unable to resolve the issue then the following options can be explored:

1. Transfer to another therapist. If you are involved with a group practice or community mental health setting you can do so within the agency.

2. You may contact the counselor's supervisor if she or he has one.

If you feel that you have been treated unethically and cannot resolve the issue with your therapist or her/his supervisor, then you may decide to contact the State Board that regulates the licensure of your therapist. There are several licenses: L.C.S.W. (licensed clinical social worker), L.P.C. (licensed professional counselor), L.M.F.T. (licensed marriage and family therapist), Psy.D. (clinical psychologist), Ph.D. (psychologist), and M.D. (psychiatrist).

Through the looking glass: A section for therapists unfamiliar with lesbians and gays

In 1973 the American Psychiatric Association declared that homosexuality was no longer considered a mental illness, and in 1975 the American Psychological Association followed suit.

Research concerning twins has shown there may be a genetic component, but not in all cases, and studies of the brain have shown some slight differences between gay and straight men. There is still no conclusive evidence on what causes sexual orientation. More and more it is thought to have a genetic component, and the fact remains that there have been gay and bisexual people throughout history.

Here is a sample of a few of the more famous lesbian and gay people: Jane Addams, Alexander the Great, Susan B. Anthony, St. Augustine, Katharine Lee Bates (who wrote "America the Beautiful"), Marie-Rosalie Bonheur, Rita Mae Brown, Michelangelo Buonarroti, Lord George Gordon Byron, Leonardo Da Vinci, Ellen DeGeneres, Emily Dickinson, King Edward II, Melissa Etheridge, Anna Freud, Radclyffe Hall, Rock Hudson, King James I, k.d. lang, Wladziu Liberace, Freddie Mercury, Harvey Milk, Martina

Navratilova, Florence Nightingale, King Richard the Lionhearted, Eleanor Roosevelt, Saints Serge and Bacchus who were joined in a holy union, Sappho, William Shakespeare, Bessie Smith, Socrates, Gertrude Stein, Peter Tchaikovsky, Alice Walker, Andy Warhol, Patricia Nell Warren, Walt Whitman, Oscar Wilde, King William II, King William III, Tennessee Williams, and Virginia Woolf.

The current literature is in agreement that homosexuality is not learned. It is commonly understood that those who are lesbian or gay are born that way. Some know all of their lives that they are homosexual, while others do not come to terms with their sexuality until later in life. Growing up is difficult for gay people. As a child there are messages from society that say it is wrong to be gay. We are still bombarded with stereotypical examples of effeminate men and masculine women. There are few positive role models for gay people, let alone children who are gay. Many gay people state that they realized they were "different" at adolescence and sometimes earlier, and some report that they were already adults before they realized their attraction for others of the same sex.

It is important to realize that not all lesbians are masculine in appearance, and that not all gay men are effeminate. Those who are "stereotypical" do not make up the entire population of gay communities. It is also important to note that lesbians do not want to be men and that gay men do not want to be women. They are simply individuals who are attracted to others of the same sex for fulfillment of affectional and sexual needs.

We have all heard the terms "dyke," "faggot," "queer," and "fairy." These terms are full of anger and intolerance. They are words that are used to hurt and demean others and to ease the fear of someone who does not understand. Society has given us the lesson that to be gay is to be an object of contempt. There is pain in being an outcast because of homophobia; therefore, some lesbians and gay men hide this aspect of themselves.

A big problem that faces gay people who are hiding their sexuality is low self-image. This is understandable when taking into account the views of society and how they are internalized. There are two coping strategies that can help in dealing with the low self-image: self-labeling as a lesbian and self-disclosure of sexual orientation to people who are supportive. These two strategies help the person to develop a positive homosexual identity. It is somewhat easier to come out now than it was in the past, but there is still the fear that a gay person's friends or family might reject them, or they might lose their employment or housing.

It is important to recognize and understand, from an ethical and humane standpoint, how therapists must acquaint themselves with community resources for their gay clients. Counselors should be sensitive to their gay clients' needs in order to help them cope with a society which mostly ostracizes them.

Here are a few of the issues which gay people can face:

1. Gay individuals can be victims of discrimination and prejudice. This includes negativity directed at a gay person, stereotyping, lack of support from peers, and discrimination in both housing and employment.

2. Dealing with family members is sometimes quite difficult. Even if a person has been honest and loving with her family her whole life, she may have problems sharing her sexuality with her parents. Common reasons for a person's silence may be fear of hurting or disappointing her parents or receiving negative reactions from them.

3. Gay clients need help with communication skills and development of a positive self-image. Substance abuse is one way gay people may learn to cope in a negative way. Also needed is a knowledge of relationship building skills, especially since society does not provide nurturance for or acknowledgment of gay relationships, including monogamous lesbian or gay partnerships which may have lasted for decades. Gay partners who seek couples counseling should be able to focus on their relationship issues rather than problems stemming from being gay in today's world.

When surveyed most therapists agree that homosexuality is not a mental illness and that gays can be as well-adjusted as heterosexuals. Many feel gays should be able to adopt children if they are "fit" parents.

It is very important for heterosexual counselors to ethically meet the needs of their gay clients by educating themselves to the terminology used, understanding that the client was born gay and that it is an orientation that cannot be changed, and to make an effort to understand that their clients have no desire to be the opposite sex. It is also important to understand that gay individuals need to deal with problems of self-esteem due to the stress and pressure our society exerts to conform to a "heterosexual norm." Such understanding may be gained by continuing education workshops, research of current literature in the field, becoming familiar with resources within the community, and becoming clear about one's own feelings toward gay women and men. If a counselor or therapist is uncomfortable with a client who is a gay person, then ethically she/he must refer the client to another therapist.

CHAPTER 6

Living in the primarily heterosexual USA

A final little soapbox

The reason I decided to include this chapter in this book is because I have had many conversations with my straight friends who have no idea how hard it is to be a gay man or woman in the United States. Most people do not realize that we basically have no rights, and that we can be freely discriminated against with no legal recourse.

The only way this will ever change is for people to realize that it is going on and decide to do something about it. We are all brothers and sisters in this world, and I believe together we can make it a much better one.

Our "civil rights" in the USA

Many people think that you cannot be discriminated against in housing, public accommodations, education, or employment if you are a gay man or woman. WRONG. I have been harassed by neighbors; told there were no vacancies at motels, even though their glaring neon sign said differently; advised not to come out on campus or I might lose my grant; and I've been fired from three jobs for being a lesbian. These things have been pretty devastating, to say the least.

I even had one employer hire a private investigator to track me. I had worked for him for over two years, and I was up for a promotion to assistant manager. When the investigator verified that I was lesbian, I was fired without notice right in the middle of the '80s recession. I went from being the head buyer for a store to squeezing dogs' anal glands in a grooming parlor, Of course my employers did not say my sexuality was the reason. No, they said I was a drug user, which was totally untrue—I don't even drink—and that I was "an unreliable employee." Hmmm. I guess never being late to work or missing a day in two years means unreliable to some people.

Now, you must remember this was in the deep South, where intolerance is a daily right to every god-fearin' homophobe, but there are people like this everywhere you go—people who are pointing one finger at you with three pointing right back at themselves!

Don't laws protect gay people from discrimination?

Not in most states, but most everyone I've spoken to thinks we are protected. An acquaintance of mine who has a doctorate said, "If I got fired I'd go to the Lambda Legal Defense and Educational Fund and get them to help me."

The Lambda Legal Defense Fund is a great organization, but there is little chance that they would be able to do anything, unless you are in one of the twenty-one states that has civil rights legislation for gay people written into their laws.

Those states are as follows: California, Colorado, Connecticut, Delaware, Hawaii, Illinois, Indiana, Maryland, Massachusetts, Minnesota, Montana, Nevada, New Hampshire, New Jersey, New Mexico, New York, Pennsylvania, Rhode Island, Vermont, Washington, Wisconsin. Of the twenty-one only Connecticut, Massachusetts, Vermont, and Wisconsin have laws which prohibit discrimination based on sexual orientation in all categories. The categories are: public employment, public accommodations, private employment, education, housing, credit, and union practices. This information was compiled from the Lambda Defense and Educational Fund website and was last updated on January 4, 2002, so it may have changed by now.

If you want to live in a state that fully protects its gay citizens, then I'd say do some research on the ones listed above to make sure that the antidiscrimination laws have not been repealed or amended. Keep in mind that the laws are not going to change ignorant, intolerant people, and if you get into a lawsuit with a private individual, you can bet it will be a nasty fight to the bitter end.

There are also cities which have their own antidiscrimination laws. To see the summary of states, cities, and counties which prohibit discrimination based on sexual orientation go out on the Web to the Lambda Legal Defense and Educational Fund.

Why aren't gay people protected?
They pay taxes too.

Good question, but I cannot answer it. All I can say is, as you read this chapter, think about the fact that we, even lesbians and gay men, are supposedly living in a "free country." Most of us work hard; make house payments or pay rent; support ourselves, pets, or kids, on salaries significantly below a "family man's" wage; and shell out much of our gross income to taxes.

The tax thing irritates me more than anything, so I am going to include a very loose approximation of how much gay people paid out in taxes for one year. The estimate was compiled from the website of the U.S. Census Bureau. The employment numbers available were for October 1, 2000. So here we go:

On October 1, 2000 there were approximately 162,410,000 people living in the USA between the ages of 20 and 64 years old (what I would consider working age). If you multiply that number by 10 percent (the low end of the approximate percentage of the population who are gay, both men and women) you get 16,241,000 gay people employed. If you take that number and multiply it by the median income (let's go way low to make up for the approximate number of gay people who may not be

> **Did You Know?**
>
> Katharine Lee Bates wrote "America the Beautiful" for the woman she had a loving relationship with for twenty-five years.

working, and say $20,000 per year) you get $324,820,000,000 in gay annual salaries, which we spend in the USA as consumers. Now multiply this by the federal tax rate of 12.5% (keep in mind, most of us pay almost 25% of our wages) and you get gay people paying $40,602,500,000 in federal income taxes per year. This does not include state or local taxes.

Now wait a minute! Gay people pay over forty BILLION dollars in federal income taxes and yet we have no rights in many of the states across the United States? What's up with that? The only right the federal government gives us is that we cannot be discriminated against in public employment; but if someone wants to fire you, believe me, they'll find a way to get around that little law. Doesn't the *Pledge of Allegiance* say "and freedom and justice for all"? I don't think that pledge means freedom and justice just for straight, white Christians, especially since this country was founded on religious freedom for all who seek it.

Now, I'm not trying to fuel the fire into a homo war, but this is just not right. I don't know what the solution is either. I did have a discussion with a black man who was running for senate in the state where I live. I told him how I felt I had no rights as a lesbian, and how I thought it was very similar to how black people had no rights just forty years ago. He sadly shook his head and replied, "The only thing I know to tell you to do is to make a stand for your own rights as an American. It's scary, but one person can make a difference." I think he was speaking from experience, being that he's black and was running for the senate in a state where many are racist.

I never forgot our little discussion, but for years I was unsure of how one person could do anything to change the way a whole country thinks. Then I read the book *Excuse Me, Your LIFE is Waiting* by Lynn Grabhorn, and my whole way of viewing things turned around. I learned that the first step to figuring out what you want life to be is to know what you don't want or what you don't have. So, with that in mind, the next section will cover the basic things some of us don't have at this time because we were born gay and not heterosexual.

The privilege of being heterosexual

There are many privileges that people automatically have for being born heterosexual. Most are just so ingrained in all of us that we don't even question their validity, that is unless these privileges are taken away by homophobia.

Heterosexual Privilege #1: Marriage

When you are in a heterosexual marriage your relationship is happily supported by society. Holidays, vacations, and celebrations are promoted by parents, in-laws, coworkers, and most people in general. What you do to celebrate these occasions can be freely discussed without fear of people scoffing at your most precious relationship.

When you are in a heterosexual marriage, you will automatically be able to sign up for certain types of insurance, such as homeowners, auto, or health at a reduced "family rate."

You will have full visitation rights in the hospital intensive care or ambulatory units, and be allowed to automatically make decisions for your spouse if she or he is incapacitated.

If your spouse becomes sick, or dies suddenly, you will

probably receive paid leave from your job, no questions asked. The joint properties will automatically be turned over to the remaining spouse under probate laws, and you will receive Social Security benefits from your spouse's fund.

If you are married you may file joint tax returns and receive tax cuts that single people or single people in a committed relationship do not have.

If your marriage ends in divorce and there are children involved, you will probably have joint child custody, or at least visitation rights to your children. You will also have legal recourse to an attorney who can handle the separation of material goods if hard feelings exist.

Heterosexual Privilege #2: Total Cultural Acceptance

You will be able to live openly with your partner without fear of being an outcast in your neighborhood, work, or social life. You can freely discuss both the good and the bad times of your relationship with support from others. If you are still in high school you can automatically use the correct pronoun for the person you are dating, and not have to lie about who you went to the movies with on Saturday night. You will not have to explain your relationship to people who are just meeting you or make up a lie about who you really are. You will not have to wait to know new acquaintances a year before you disclose who your life partner is. You will not have to fear their possible rejection. You will not have to worry about speaking to children in your neighborhood, for fear that their parents may be thinking you are trying to change them into something they may or may not already be, or trying to molest them. You will not have to be afraid for your life when walking to your car outside of the bar of your peers. You will not have to worry that homosexuals will come into the bar of your peers and harass or stare at you, come onto you, or cruise the parking lots outside and dent your car or slice the tires. You will not have to worry that if you tell someone you are heterosexual they could kidnap you from wherever you are, and beat, rape, or kill you.

Heterosexual Privilege #3: Being Viewed as "Normal"

Your whole life is not tainted by the nagging wonder of what might happen if so-and-so finds out? You will have wonderful role models in movies, on television, and in books that will teach you about romance and give you a very good idea of what a healthy heterosexual relationship is. You will be bombarded non-stop through the media with people you can identify with. You will not ever have to question your sexuality in relation to what society deems correct.

Heterosexual Privilege #4: Total Acceptance by Employers, Church, and State

If you are heterosexual, you will not have to worry about disclosing who you are in an interview for fear of not being hired. You will not have to guard your personal life fiercely, having little contact with coworkers and not attending company social activities in order to protect you job. You will not have to lie about who your beneficiary is on your life insurance policy, or choose a family member instead of the person you live with. You will not have to be on guard any time you are anywhere with your partner, for fear someone from work will see you and label you as a homosexual. You will not have to say your heterosexual boyfriend, girlfriend, wife or husband is "your friend," when introducing them to people from your work. You will not have to worry about displaying affection to your significant other in public. You can openly have a job as a minister or a teacher without the constant worry of being humiliated and fired if your private life is discovered. You may openly adopt or provide foster care to children. In a divorce situation you can raise your own children without the constant threat that your ex will regain custody in a court of law because of who you love. You will not have to hide your relationship from the police if your children get in trouble. You will be able to openly serve in the military.

Heterosexism, a right of the majority?

At present, heterosexism is everywhere we look. From TV to billboards to advertising on the radio, we are constantly bombarded with heterosexual imagery, and yet many of us are still gay. Much time and research has been done on the question of human sexuality, and we are still shrugging our shoulders and scratching our heads.

Several years ago a questionnaire was distributed in hopes of getting answers to the age-old question, "What makes a person gay?" Following is the lesbian version of that questionnaire.

Heterosexual, choice or not?

1. How old were you when you decided you were going to be a heterosexual?

2. Deep down inside, what do you believe converted you into a heterosexual?

3. Do you think you may grow out of being a heterosexual?

4. How do you know for sure that you are heterosexual if you have never had sexual relations with someone of your own sex?

5. Do you have a deep-seated fear of lesbians and gay

men which causes you to be heterosexual?

6. Even though it is a fact that most child molesters are heterosexuals, do you still feel it is OK for your children to be taught by heterosexual teachers?

7. Even though society supports heterosexual marriage, it ends in divorce nearly 50 percent of the time. Why aren't heterosexuals content with their "preferred" lifestyle?

8. Do you believe you could be influenced and become a lesbian or a gay man?

9. Do you think you will ever be a complete human being by limiting yourself and your sexuality to being only heterosexual?

10. Even though their lives will be plagued with problems, would you still want your children to be heterosexual?

11. Since most heterosexuals are so unhappy with their chosen lifestyle, perhaps some type of aversion therapy may help those who really want to become a happy, productive, well-rounded person.

Hopefully, this chapter has helped you to understand how hard it can be when you are a gay woman or man. I know sometimes it is easier to ignore the problems of prejudice in this culture, but that will not make them go away. The only way for change to happen is if we realize that there is something desperately wrong with how at least 10 percent of the population is being treated, and make a step for positive change. We need to stop judging each other, and take back the control of our thoughts, feelings, and lives instead.

Many of my straight friends have no idea how hard it can be to live as a gay person today. They think because Ellen had a TV show that everything is fine concerning gays and society. Many think because they accept us, everyone else will, which leads to them possibly blurting out that a friend is gay in the breakroom at work or the classroom at school. Most people either do not understand the prejudices and intolerances that we face on a daily basis, or, because of heterosexual privilege, it just never crossed their minds.

The thing I have found that works best is to openly discuss unfair situations with my supportive straight friends. I always make sure to tell them that it has been my experience that not everyone views lesbians and gays in a nice way. Some people can become so threatened that they could cause a person to lose her job or even her housing.

I always work on helping my heterosexual friends understand that all is not bright and sunny on the homo side of the fence, and that we have plenty of sharp rocks and weeds to pull out before there are green pastures for us. I've found that being honest about the prejudice I have experienced has helped my straight friends change into supporters who will stand up for the rights of all gay people, not tolerate lesbian or gay jokes or slurs, and basically dig up a hidden cactus before I even come close to stepping on it.

A happy ending

I hope this little book will help you in your quest to become the greatest lover you can be.

This is a new millennium, full of the promise of freedom and equality for us all, and I wish you the happiest, most wonderful future you could ever imagine.

Tracey Stevens

Bibliography

Want to get there fast?
You can find live links to these books and websites at
http://www.amazingdreamspublishing.com/hlbiblio.html

Reference Books

Bass, Ellen; Davis, Laura, *The Courage to Heal, A Guide for Women Survivors of Child Sexual Abuse*, New York: Harper & Row, Publishers, 1994.

Bradshaw, John, *Homecoming, Reclaiming and Championing Your Inner Child*, New York: Bantam Books, 1992.

Davis, Laura, *The Courage to Heal Workbook, For Women and Men Survivors of Child Sexual Abuse*, New York: Harper & Row, Publishers, 1990.

Grabhorn, Lynn, *Excuse Me, Your LIFE Is Waiting*, Virginia: Hampton Roads Publishing Company, Inc., 2000.

Koop, C. Everett, M.D., *Dr. Koop's Self-Care Advisor*, California: Time Life Medical, The Health Publishing Group, 1996.

Komaroff, Anthony L., M.D., *Harvard Medical School Family Health Guide*, New York: Simon & Schuster, 1999.

Masters, William H.; Johnson, Virginia E.; Kolodny, Robert C., Human Sexuality 4th Edition, New York: Harper Collins, 1992.

Sisley, Emily L., M.D.; Harris, Bertha, *The Joy of Lesbian Sex*, New York: Simon & Schuster, 1977.

West, Celeste, *A Lesbian Love Advisor*, Pennsylvania: Cleis Press, 1989.

Westheimer, Ruth, M.D., *Sex for Dummies*, California: IDG Books Worldwide Inc., 1995.

Resources

Want to get there fast?
You can find live links to these books and websites at
http://www.amazingdreamspublishing.com/hlbiblio.html

Helping your family understand:

Parents, Families and Friends of Lesbians and Gays (PFLAG)
1726 M Street, NW, Suite 400, Washington, DC 20036,
202-467-8180
PFLAG'S easy-to-use website has lots of information
and lists local chapters by state: http://www.pflag.org/
email: info@pflag.org

With 488 chapters reaching over 80,000 households, Parents, Families and Friends of Lesbians and Gays (PFLAG) helps gay, lesbian, bisexual, and transgendered (GLBT) people, their families and friends, through support, education, and advocacy. PFLAG's line of publications addresses a variety of support and educational issues for both GLBT people and allies. Their publications help prepare families and friends for the challenges of supporting GLBT loved ones. PFLAG's mission promotes the health and well-being of gay, lesbian, bisexual, and transgendered persons, and their families and friends through: support, to cope with an adverse society; education, to enlighten an ill-informed public; and advocacy, to end discrimination and secure equal civil rights. PFLAG provides opportunities for dialogue about sexual orientation and gender identity, and acts to create a society that is healthy and respectful of human diversity.

Books to help your parents, family, and friends:

Beyond Acceptance: Parents of Lesbians and Gays Talk About Their Experiences by Carolyn Welch Griffin, Marian J. Wirth, Arthur G. Wirth, Brian McNaught, December 1997, St. Martin's Press; ISBN: 0312167814

Coming Out as Parents: You and Your Homosexual Child
by David K. Switzer, September 1996, Westminster John Knox
Press; ISBN: 0664256368

*Is It a Choice?: Answers to 300 of the Most Frequently Asked
Questions About Gay and Lesbian People* by Eric Marcus,
June 1999, Harper San Francisco; ISBN: 006251623X

My Child Is Gay: How Parents React When They Hear the News
by Bryce McDougall (Editor), October 1998, Allen & Unwin;
ISBN: 1864486589

*Outing Yourself: How to Come Out as Lesbian or Gay to Your
Family, Friends, and Coworkers* by Michelangelo Signorile,
June 1996, Fireside; ISBN: 0684826178

*Straight Parents, Gay Children: Inspiring Families to Live
Honestly and With Greater Understanding* by Robert A.
Bernstein, May 1999, Thunder's Mouth Press; ISBN:
1560252294

Where to go for help if you've been sexually abused:

The Rape, Abuse & Incest National Network (RAINN)

635-B Pennsylvania Ave. SE, Washington, DC 20003,
1-800-656-4673
http://www.rainn.org/

RAINN is a nonprofit organization based in Washington, DC that
operates a national hotline for survivors of sexual assault. The
hotline offers free, confidential counseling from anywhere in the
country. You can call the RAINN hotline 24 hours a day at 1-800-
656-HOPE, or you can locate a crisis center near you by using their
search function on their website. RAINN is provided as a service
for survivors who cannot reach a rape crisis center through a local
call. Currently, the majority of the country is a toll call away from
a rape crisis center. Many of these long distance callers are being
abused by someone in their own household and thus can't utilize a
service that will appear on a phone bill.

Online support for victims of domestic partner abuse; childhood psychological, physical or sexual abuse; rape and hate crimes:

Rainbow Hope

http://www.rainbowhope.org

We support lesbians who were abused (psychological, physical or sexual) in their childhoods, who were raped, who were victims of hate crimes or of domestic violence. This site was created so that we could share our experiences, grief, hopes, struggles and dreams. We wanted to create a space where women could be themselves without the fear of being judged because of sexual orientation issues. We hope that we can provide you with a safe place to finally be able to be completely yourself.

Breaking The Silence

http://t.webring.com/hub?ring=survivors

Open to everyone; age, gender, background irrelevant. Survivors of sexual and gender violence, rape, sexual abuse, harassment, FGM and GLBT hate crimes. Most are against women by men, but we don't seek to exclude male survivors or victims of female assailants. Sites in the web ring are by or about survivors and most include resources or inspiration in coping with surviving. Our motto is: "Work for survival, and refuse to keep the secrets of the crimes we have suffered." By sharing our pain, we are sharing our strengths.

Friendly places to buy books and videos
TLA Video

TLA Entertainment Group, 234 Market Street, Philadelphia, PA 19106, 215-733-0608

http://www.tlavideo.com

Store Locations:
South Street-Society Hill, 517 S. 4th Street, Philadelphia, PA 19147, 215-922-3838

Chestnut Hill, 7630 Germantown Avenue, Philadelphia PA 19118, 215-248-4448

Rittenhouse Square, 1520 Locust Street, Philadelphia, PA 19102, 215-735-7887

Bryn Mawr, 763 Lancaster Avenue, Bryn Mawr, PA 19010, 610-520-1222

Art Museum, 1808 Spring Garden Street, Philadelphia, PA 19130, 215-751-1171

West Village, Manhattan, 52-54 West 8th Street, New York, NY 10001, 212-228-8282

Toys, safer sex items, and other stuff for women

Good Vibrations
http://www.goodvibes.com/
e-mail: goodvibe@well.com

Good Vibrations is a women-owned and women-operated cooperative which has been promoting sexual health and pleasure since 1977. From a great antique vibrator online museum to toys for the new millennium, Good Vibrations has it all. Books, audio, video, and even a section to "Get Off Cheap" are included in their great website.

Good Vibrations San Fransisco, 1210 Valencia Street (@ 23rd Street), San Francisco, CA 94110, 415-974-8980

Good Vibrations Berkeley Store, 2504 San Pablo Avenue (@ Dwight), Berkeley, CA 94702, 510-841-8987

To order a catalog by phone, call: 800-289-8423

Toys in Babeland
http://www.babeland.com
e-mail: mailorder@babeland.com

Toys in Babeland is the famously fun lesbian-owned, women-run adult toy store in Seattle, New York and online at Babeland.com. Find the gear, guidance, and inspiration for a satisfying love life with the help of their staff educators. Visitors to Seattle and New

York should check out the events listings on their website for their unique in-store workshops: "Babeland University."

New York, Toys in Babeland, 94 Rivington Street
(between Orchard and Ludlow),
New York, NY 10002, 212-375-1701

Seattle, Toys in Babeland, 707 E. Pike Street,
Seattle, WA 98122, 206-328-2914.

To order a catalog by phone: 800-658-9119

Internet hosting

kryss.com
http://www.kryss.com/

"Looking for award-winning website design, a webmaster to help you maintain your site, an e-commerce package that ROCKS, or a great place to get affordable web hosting? At kryss.com, we aim for 100% customer satisfaction. We have lightning fast, reliable servers, connections, service, and support. We are also well-known for including more features with our virtual hosting package than many hosts charging two to five times more. Check out our Hosting Comparison page to see why you should choose kryss.com as your web presence provider."

Electronic cards

Free nonpornographic e-cards for and by women
http://www.amazingdreamspublishing.com/ecards.html